Beginning BlackBerry Development

Anthony Rizk

apress®

Beginning BlackBerry Development

ISBN-13 (pbk): 978-1-4302-2427-3

ISBN-13 (electronic): 978-1-4302-2428-0

Trademarked names may appear in this book. Rather than use a trademark symbol with every occurrence of a trademarked name, we use the names only in an editorial fashion and to the benefit of the trademark owner, with no intention of infringement of the trademark.

Lead Editor: Ewan Buckingham
Technical Reviewer: Paul Dumais
Editorial Board: Clay Andres, Steve Anglin, Mark Beckner, Ewan Buckingham, Tony Campbell, Gary Cornell, Jonathan Gennick, Michelle Lowman, Matthew Moodie, Jeffrey Pepper, Frank Pohlmann, Ben Renow-Clarke, Dominic Shakeshaft, Matt Wade, Tom Welsh
Coordinating Editor: Anne Collett
Copy Editors: Heather Lang, Ginny Munroe and Kim Wimpsett
Compositor: MacPS, LLC
Indexer: BIM Indexing and e-Services
Artist: April Milne

Distributed to the book trade worldwide by Springer-Verlag New York, Inc., 233 Spring Street, 6th Floor, New York, NY 10013. Phone 1-800-SPRINGER, fax 201-348-4505, e-mail orders-ny@springer-sbm.com, or visit http://www.springeronline.com.

For information on translations, please e-mail info@apress.com, or visit http://www.apress.com.

Apress and friends of ED books may be purchased in bulk for academic, corporate, or promotional use. eBook versions and licenses are also available for most titles. For more information, reference our Special Bulk Sales–eBook Licensing web page at http://www.apress.com/info/bulksales.

The information in this book is distributed on an "as is" basis, without warranty. Although every precaution has been taken in the preparation of this work, neither the author(s) nor Apress shall have any liability to any person or entity with respect to any loss or damage caused or alleged to be caused directly or indirectly by the information contained in this work.

The source code for this book is available to readers at http://www.apress.com. You will need to answer questions pertaining to this book in order to successfully download the code.

To Sabrina and Hannah
–Anthony

Contents at a Glance

Contents

About the Author

 **Anthony Rizk** is an experienced mobile application developer; he is currently CTO and co-founder of Zeebu Mobile, which makes educational mobile applications for children. Previously, Anthony was a founding member of Rove Mobile where he was part of the team that created and developed their mobile network management products, including Mobile Admin, Mobile SSH, and PCMobilizr. He has been developing BlackBerry applications for over 8 years and has consulted extensively in the wireless application industry. He lives in Ottawa with his wife and daughter.

About the Technical Reviewer

 **Paul Dumais** is a mobile application innovator; he is currently the Senior Technical Architect for BlackBerry App World at Research In Motion. Previously, Paul co-founded Rove Mobile (formerly Idokorro) where he was responsible for creating and developing all their mobile network management products including Mobile Admin, Mobile SSH, Mobile Desktop, Mobile Citrix, BlackBerry Viewer and PCMobilizr. His expertise includes developing applications for BlackBerry, Symbian, Windows Mobile, Palm and iPhone. In 1999, Paul created an award winning change management product that was acquired by MKS which is now serving as the foundation of the MKS Integrity Platform.

Acknowledgments

Thank you to the two most important people in my life, without whom this book would not have been written: My wife, Sabrina, for encouraging my writing in blog and book form, keeping me away from distractions, making sure I stuck to my schedule, and taking care of our daughter on those crucial days when I needed an extra few hours to complete a chapter. My daughter Hannah for motivating me to try something new, and for still being young enough to go to bed early giving daddy a bit more time to work.

Thanks to my technical reviewer, and the best software developer I know, Paul Dumais for believing in the idea of this book from the beginning; reviewing, correcting and improving all my code; and providing ideas and information about BlackBerry development.

Thanks to the people at Research In Motion and elsewhere who provided feedback and helped improve the book, notably Mike Kirkup and his team.

Finally, thank you to the team at Apress. Anne Collett, for managing to keep the whole project to a very tight schedule, while dealing with the last minute revisions and questions of a first-time author. Ewan Buckingham for his editing and encouragement. Mark Beckner for bringing me into this mess in the first place. Finally Heather Lang, Ginny Munroe, and Kim Wimpsett for such a fantastic job copy editing. My first book has been a fun and eye-opening experience thanks to all of you.

Chapter 1

Setting the Stage

There has never been a better time to develop applications for BlackBerry devices than right now. Since Research In Motion (RIM) launched the first models almost a decade ago, the BlackBerry smartphone has gone from relative obscurity to near universal visibility—think about how commonplace it has become to see people in airports, hotels, offices, or just about anywhere stealing a few minutes to check their e-mail or type replies. The BlackBerry software development kit has been around since the first devices were released and has grown to include an extensive collection of examples, documentation, and a mature set of APIs and tools that have opened the door for all kinds of great applications, most of which only currently exist in someone's imagination. And with the maturing of the BlackBerry community and the introduction of BlackBerry App World, it's easier than ever to get your application noticed and downloaded by users worldwide.

In this chapter we'll talk a bit about the basics of BlackBerry development –development environment options (there are a couple), other software and information you need, and some things to keep in mind. We'll also walk through the download and setup of the development tools and simulators so we're all set up to start building applications in the next chapter. What This Book Is

This book is a guide to help you get started creating your own BlackBerry applications. This book is not about writing web applications for BlackBerry devices or about rapid application development (RAD) solutions, such as MDS Studio or the BlackBerry Plug-in for Microsoft Visual Studio. This is about building professional, polished, native applications that take full advantage of the BlackBerry platform.

By the end of this book, you'll have built several simple BlackBerry applications, learned how to run them on the various BlackBerry simulators, and how to package and deploy them onto real BlackBerry devices. You'll learn how a BlackBerry application is put together, how to create great looking user interfaces, how to interact with the user (using the keyboard and trackball/trackpad or touch screen depending on the device), how to send and receive data over the wireless network, and more. Combined with the extensive development resources and examples provided by RIM you'll be on your way to creating the next killer application for this platform.

What You Need to Know Before You Can Begin

To be able to follow along, you should have previous programming experience in a modern object-oriented language. This book is not an introduction to object-oriented programming, or even to the Java language. There are many excellent resources and tutorials available on the internet.

BlackBerry applications are written in Java Micro Edition (Java ME) formerly called J2ME. This is a subset of Java Standard Edition (Java SE) that most Java developers work with. If you're familiar with Java SE or Java Enterprise Edition (Java EE), Java ME will be very easy to pick up.

If you're familiar with another object-oriented language – especially one with a similar syntax like C#, C++ or even Objective-C – you should similarly have no problem picking things up. C# developers in particular should be able to understand Java ME code with little or no effort.

One of the nice things about Java ME and the BlackBerry from the perspective of a beginner is that the API is small compared to desktop or server programming environments – you can learn a great deal of it fairly quickly. Of course, this is a double-edged sword; there will be times you wish the API provided some functionality that bigger environments do, though the BlackBerry API is getting more functionality all the time.

Setting Up Your Development Environment

Before you can begin writing applications for BlackBerry you'll need a few things. First, you'll need a computer running Windows 2000 SP1 or later, Windows XP, or Windows Vista. Any desktop or laptop produced in the last few years should be sufficient, but as with any software development, the more RAM and CPU speed you have, the better your experience will be.

The first stop for all BlackBerry development tools and other resources is the BlackBerry Developer Zone at http://www.blackberry.com/developers/. See Figure 1-1. Here, you'll find free downloads, whitepapers, the developer knowledge base, and the BlackBerry Developer Forums. As a BlackBerry developer, you should get to know this site very well.

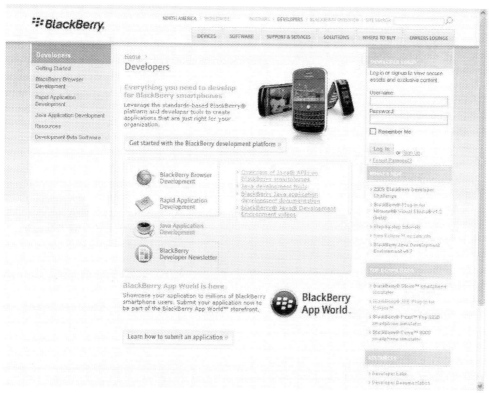

Figure 1-1. *The BlackBerry Developer Zone*

While you're looking at this page, you might as well sign up for a developer account – it's free and quick, and you'll need a login to download the developer tools.

RIM does offer higher-level paid developer programs with additional support and other benefits, but you can develop and distribute applications with the free account.

Installing the Development Environment

There are two BlackBerry development environments produced by RIM. The BlackBerry Java Development Environment (JDE), and the BlackBerry JDE Plug-in for Eclipse. Both are very functional and have been used by developers to produce professional applications. The JDE has been around longer and is a bit more mature, but almost everything possible with the JDE can also be accomplished with the Eclipse Plug-in. The Eclipse Plug-in leverages the entire Eclipse development platform, which includes a world-class source code editor and a lot of third-party plug-ins. Ultimately, the choice is a matter of personal preference. We'll explore both in the next chapter, so you'll get a better idea of what the real-world differences are. There are no issues with installing both the JDE and the JDE Plug-in for Eclipse on the same computer, so if you're interested in exploring both and don't mind the extra time and effort, feel free to follow through the install instructions for both later in this chapter.

After deciding between the JDE and the JDE Plug-in, you'll need to decide on a JDE version. Each version of the JDE (or each version of the component pack for the Eclipse Plug-in) corresponds to a major version of the BlackBerry operating system (OS). BlackBerry does a good job of keeping their OS backward compatible, so something developed for OS 4.2 generally will work the same on OS 4.3 and higher. However, you may want to use some features that are only available in a later OS. A safe minimum is 4.2, which covers all trackball devices and later and is the minimum version supported by BlackBerry App World.

The one exception to all of this is the touch screen BlackBerry Storm, which runs OS 4.7 and can be temperamental with applications built using older versions of the JDE. You can run applications compiled with versions of the JDE earlier than JDE v4.7 on the Storm, and they will work. However, by default, they'll be run in Compatibility Mode, meaning the user experience won't be ideal. To avoid Compatibility Mode, you must compile your application with JDE v4.7 or higher. In many cases, you can just recompile the same source code.

The bottom line is that if you're planning on targeting the Storm, you should be sure to get the JDE or JDE Plug-in v4.7 in addition to any other versions.

Before installing the BlackBerry development tools, you'll need to install the Java SE JDK from http://java.sun.com. The version or versions you will have to install depends on the version of the BlackBerry platform you want to target. For most developers, downloading Java SE JDK v6.0 is a good choice – it will let you develop for BlackBerry Device Software version 4.2 and later, which covers all BlackBerry devices introduced in the last three years or so. More specific information is available on the Developer Zone at http://na.blackberry.com/eng/developers/javaappdev/javadevenv.jsp.

Installing the BlackBerry JDE

The JDE is a fully integrated stand-alone environment, so if you have the appropriate version of the Java Development Kit (JDK) installed, you just need to download the appropriate version of the JDE installer and run it. Everything you need for BlackBerry development is included in the JDE – from writing code using the built-in editor, to debugging using the array of BlackBerry device simulators available, to building and signing your application for deployment onto real devices. Figure 1-2 shows the BlackBerry JDE as it will appear after being launched for the first time.

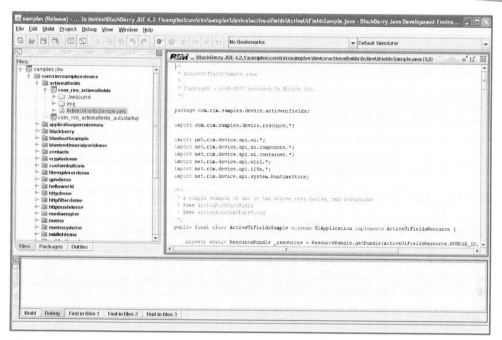

Figure 1-2. *The BlackBerry JDE v4.2.1 with the excellent (included) Samples workspace loaded, and a Java source file opened for editing*

Other JDE Versions

Each JDE version is a completely different package, so if you want to specifically target different versions of the BlackBerry API, you'll need to download more than one JDE version. Fortunately, the JDE project and workspace descriptor files will work across all current versions of the JDE, so you can open the same project in different versions.

Installing the BlackBerry JDE Plug-in for Eclipse

Obviously, you'll need to download the Eclipse integrated development environment (IDE) from http://www.eclipse.org. You need version 3.4 (Ganymede), which is shown in Figure 1-3, but beyond that any of the Java Eclipse packages will do – you only need the basic Eclipse IDE for Java Developers, but if you want the additional Java EE features, they won't affect the BlackBerry JDE Plug-in. If you already have Eclipse version 3.4 installed, you can use that as well.

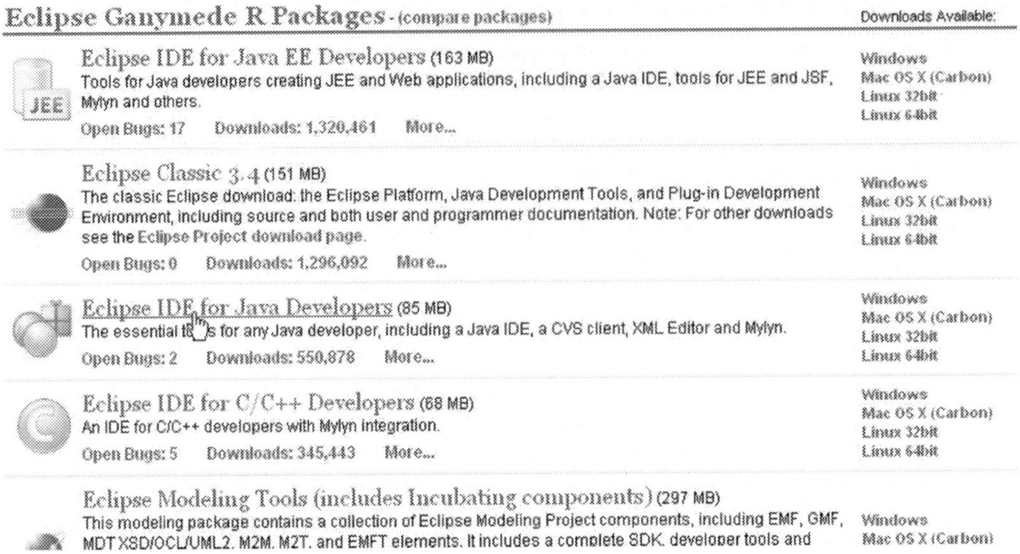

Eclipse Ganymede R Packages - (compare packages)

Eclipse IDE for Java EE Developers (163 MB)
Tools for Java developers creating JEE and Web applications, including a Java IDE, tools for JEE and JSF, Mylyn and others.
Open Bugs: 17   Downloads: 1,320,461   More...

Downloads Available:
Windows
Mac OS X (Carbon)
Linux 32bit
Linux 64bit

Eclipse Classic 3.4 (151 MB)
The classic Eclipse download: the Eclipse Platform, Java Development Tools, and Plug-in Development Environment, including source and both user and programmer documentation. Note: For other downloads see the Eclipse Project download page.
Open Bugs: 0   Downloads: 1,296,092   More...

Windows
Mac OS X (Carbon)
Linux 32bit
Linux 64bit

Eclipse IDE for Java Developers (85 MB)
The essential tools for any Java developer, including a Java IDE, a CVS client, XML Editor and Mylyn.
Open Bugs: 2   Downloads: 550,878   More...

Windows
Mac OS X (Carbon)
Linux 32bit
Linux 64bit

Eclipse IDE for C/C++ Developers (68 MB)
An IDE for C/C++ developers with Mylyn integration.
Open Bugs: 5   Downloads: 345,443   More...

Windows
Mac OS X (Carbon)
Linux 32bit
Linux 64bit

Eclipse Modeling Tools (includes Incubating components) (297 MB)
This modeling package contains a collection of Eclipse Modeling Project components, including EMF, GMF, MDT XSD/OCL/UML2, M2M, M2T, and EMFT elements. It includes a complete SDK, developer tools and

Windows
Mac OS X (Carbon)

Figure 1-3. *These are some of the available Eclipse packages. If you don't already have Eclipse installed, choose Eclipse IDE for Java Developers.*

Eclipse setup is simply a matter of unzipping the file to your PC.

Once you've gotten Eclipse set up, download the JDE Plug-in installer and run it. It includes the JDE v4.5 component pack by default.

Using Other JDE Versions with Eclipse

Other JDE versions are supported within the same environment with downloadable component packs. To install other component packs for Eclipse, download the appropriate zip file corresponding to your component pack from the BlackBerry Developer Zone, and from the Eclipse IDE choose Help ➤ Software Updates, and click the Available Software tab (see Figure 1-4).

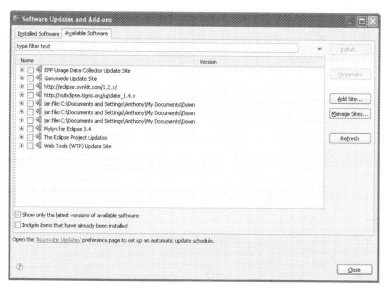

Figure 1-4. *The Eclipse software updates dialog is accessible from by choosing Software Updates from the Help menu.*

Under the Available Software tab, click Add Site. Then, click Archive, and browse for your zip file (see Figure 1-5).

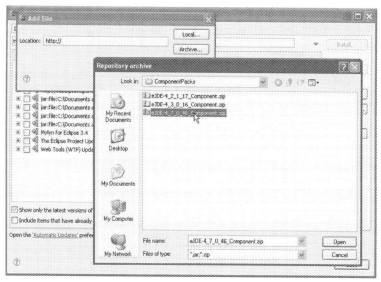

Figure 1-5. *Select Add Site and then Archive to browse to your component pack.*

Make sure the check boxes appropriate to the component pack are checked in the tree view, and click Install to continue (see Figure 1-6).

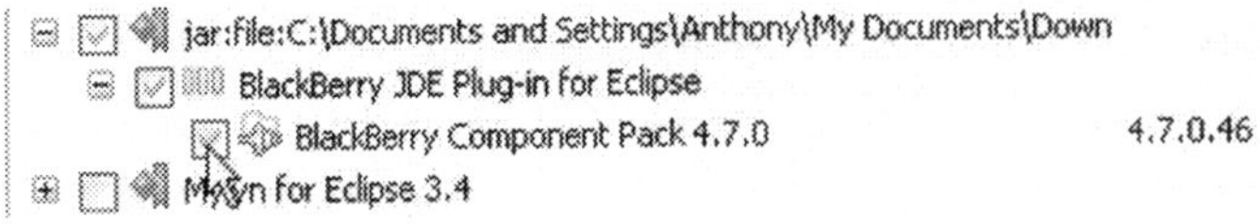

☐ ☑ ◀ jar:file:C:\Documents and Settings\Anthony\My Documents\Down
   ☐ ☑ ▣ BlackBerry JDE Plug-in for Eclipse
      ☑ ◈ BlackBerry Component Pack 4.7.0   4.7.0.46
☐ ☐ ◀ Maven for Eclipse 3.4

Figure 1-6. *Make sure all the check boxes for your archive are checked before clicking Install.*

Follow the install wizard, and your component pack will be available for use.

Downloading Additional Simulators

Each version of the JDE and version of the JDE component pack comes with a set of default simulators configured to work with the environment. RIM provides many more simulators, however. These are very useful for testing how your application functions with different screen resolutions or input methods. The simulators can be downloaded from the Developer Zone at `http://na.blackberry.com/eng/developers/resources/simulators.jsp` (see Figure 1-7 for a sample list).

Make sure to download simulators that correspond with your JDE or JDE Plug-in Component pack version.

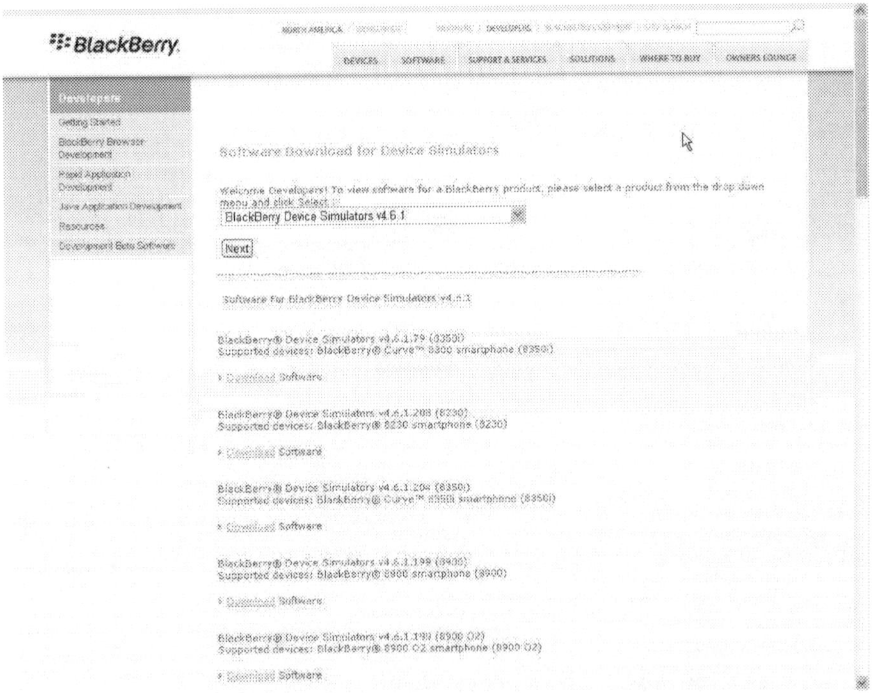

Figure 1-7. *The Simulators Download page showing some of the many choices*

Installing Desktop Software

If you want to load your application onto a BlackBerry device directly from your computer (i.e., without having to upload to a web server and download to your device over the wireless connection), you'll need to install the BlackBerry Desktop Manager (see Figure 1-8), which includes the device drivers for the BlackBerry. You may already have this installed, since it comes on a CD with your device or. you can downloade it from http://www.blackberry.com. You'll also need this to be able to debug your application on a device using your USB cable.

Figure 1-8. *You can use the BlackBerry Desktop Manager to load applications from your computer to your device.*

Getting Code Signing Keys

For basic applications, you can compile and run on real BlackBerry devices with no further involvement from RIM using the free tools. However, if you want to use certain features (such as the BlackBerry persistent store, cryptography APIs, and embeddable web browser) or if you want to allow your application to do things like automatically start, you'll need code signing keys from RIM. The code signing keys are only required to use controlled APIs from an application running on a device; you can run an application on the simulator that uses controlled APIs without having to sign it.

Since code signing keys usually only take a day or two to receive and a set of keys is only $20, it's a good idea to get them while you're setting up your development environment—almost every BlackBerry application ends up needing to use at least a few controlled APIs.

You can find more information and register for the code signing keys at `http://na.blackberry.com/eng/developers/javaappdev/codekeys.jsp`.

The online application form for signing keys is available at `https://www.blackberry.com/SignedKeys/`.

When filling in the key request form, remember the PIN you choose. You'll need it to install the keys into your JDE. Because it's sometimes a point of confusion, it's worth pointing out that your signing key PIN is not related to a BlackBerry device PIN in any way.

Installing Your Code Signing Keys

Once you've applied for your signing keys, you should receive three e-mails from RIM, each containing one of the code signing keys. Each gives access to a different part of the API, and you should install all three on the same PC. Follow the steps in this section for each of the three keys.

If you've installed the JDE, the appropriate file associations will have been made during install, and you can just double-click each of the keys to start the registration process. From the JDE Plug-in for Eclipse, select Install Signature Keys from the BlackBerry menu. Both methods will look the same from this point onwards.

> **NOTE:** Because the key database format sometimes changes, you should install using the earliest version of the JDE or JDE Plug-in you have and copy the key database to later versions as outlined later in this section.

If this is the first of the three keys you've installed, you'll be prompted to create a new public/private key pair (see Figure 1-9).

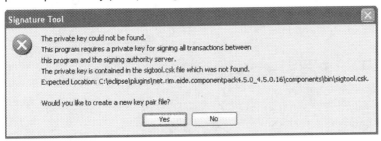

Figure 1-9. *When installing your first key, you'll be prompted to create a new key pair.*

Click Yes in this dialog, and you'll be asked for a private key password to protect your key file. *Remember this password* – you'll be asked for it *every* time you want to sign your application. You'll then be asked to generate some random data by moving your mouse pointer around (see Figure 1-10). A word of warning: this will seem like more fun than it should.

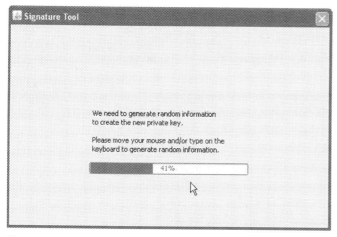

Figure 1-10. *Generating random information for your new key pair—whee!*

After this, you'll be asked to enter the PIN you provided when you applied for your keys, and the private key password you just entered (see Figure 1-11). Do this, and your key will be installed and ready to use.

Figure 1-11. *Registering a code signing key with the JDE*

For the next two keys, you'll already have generated your key pair, so you'll just have to enter the PIN and private key password.

Installing the Signing Keys for Different JDE Versions

Once you've created your key pair and installed your three keys, you'll probably want them to be available for each version of the JDE or JDE Plug-in Component Pack you have installed. The key information is stored in three files:

    sigtool.csk
    sigtool.db
    sigtool.set

These are located in the following default locations; make the appropriate substitutions for JDE version and nondefault install locations on your system:

For the JDE: `C:\Program Files\Research In Motion\BlackBerry JDE 4.2.1\bin`

For the JDE Plug-In for Eclipse:
`C:\eclipse\plugins\net.rim.eide.componentpack4.2.1_4.2.1.17\ components\bin`

To make your keys available for different JDE or JDE Plug-in Component pack versions, simply copy these files into the appropriate bin directory. It's also a very good idea to keep a backup of these files and your original key files if you ever have to rebuild your development environment.

What's Different About Developing for BlackBerry

If you're familiar with developing for modern desktop PCs or servers, there are many things you might not think about before starting to develop for BlackBerry. Of course, every platform is different, but there are some things to keep in mind when designing and implementing an application for BlackBerry.

Limited CPU and Memory

Generally, BlackBerry CPU speed and RAM – as with most mobile devices – lag a few years behind average PCs. The latest BlackBerry devices are getting faster, so this isn't as much of a constraint as it was a few years ago. There are lots of reasons for these limitations, including prolonging battery life and keeping devices small, but in general, it's good to keep in mind that your processor-intensive desktop application algorithm may not run as nicely on a BlackBerry device. Ways around this include redesigning your application to let the server, if you have one, do some of the heavy lifting.

Also, because the BlackBerry OS is multitasking, CPU- or RAM-hungry applications running in the background can make things difficult for other applications on the device. This is another way of saying "play nice with other applications on the device!"

Java as the Native API

The Java virtual machine (VM) on the BlackBerry is as close to the hardware as you can get. You can't write a non-Java native application for the platform. This means that you're always in a garbage-collected, bytecode-interpreted environment, and you don't have real-time access to the hardware.

Limited Screen Real-Estate

The largest BlackBerry device screen, in terms of number of pixels and physical size, is the touch-screen Storm. It measures 3.25 inches and has a 360 × 480 resolution. Most devices have a 3-inch or smaller screen.

User Input

The BlackBerry Storm lets the user click anywhere on the screen. Other devices don't have a touch screen, so the user is limited to the trackball (or trackpad on some recent device models) and keyboard. The trackball is like a set of up, down, left, and right cursor keys—not like a mouse. Your user interface must be designed with this in mind. Imagine how difficult it would be to navigate around a modern Windows application (like Microsoft Office) using just your cursor keys, and you'll have an idea of what the BlackBerry constraints mean.

Many Different Devices

A range of BlackBerry devices is currently being sold and used, and their screen resolutions range from 240 × 260 to 480 × 360. Physical screen sizes change too.

Some of the devices have a trackball or optical trackpad along with a keyboard, but a couple of models have a touch screen instead. Some have full QWERTY keyboards, while others have the BlackBerry SureType keyboard, which has one or two letters per key. The BlackBerry Storm can present different types of virtual keyboards depending on device orientation and user preferences.

Processor speed and RAM vary from device to device, as does network speed. And some hardware features, such as GPS, are not available on all devices.

You should be aware of these differences and design your application to work with as many devices as possible if you want to reach a significant number of BlackBerry users.

What's in This Book

Here's a brief overview of the remaining chapters in this book

Chapter 2

In this chapter, you'll learn how to build a simple BlackBerry application using the BlackBerry JDE and the JDE Plug-in for Eclipse. We'll debug the application using the simulator and on a real device.

Chapter 3

This chapter will discuss a number of concepts and topics important to BlackBerry applications in general, laying down some groundwork to help you understand the rest of the chapters.

Chapter 4

In this chapter, you'll start to explore the user interface API in depth by building an application that supports multiple screens and a variety of different user interface controls.

Chapter 5

We'll modify the application from Chapter 4 by creating and extending a number of user interface components, and you'll learn how to work with the user interface model and create a custom look and feel for your applications.

Chapter 6

Next, we'll move beyond the user interface. You'll learn how to persistently store data on the device between invocations of the application or resets of the device. We'll also explore the BlackBerry file system.

Chapter 7

This chapter will explore wireless networking by creating an application that interacts with a web service on the internet.

Chapter 8

In Chapter 8, we'll explore the location-based services support on the BlackBerry platform by creating an application that gets location information using the GPS hardware in a BlackBerry smartphone and interacts with BlackBerry maps to display location information.

Chapter 9

In this chapter we'll discuss how to package and distribute your application, both from your own website and through other means. We'll talk in depth about BlackBerry App World and how to leverage its features and then briefly discuss some third-party application stores.

Chapter 10

Chapter 10 will provide a few final bits of information and a list of BlackBerry development resources that you can use to help answer your future questions...

Chapter 2

Hello World

In this chapter, you'll learn about the basics of BlackBerry application development by creating a simple Hello World application in both the BlackBerry JDE and the BlackBerry JDE Plug-in for Eclipse. The code will be the same for both—in fact, throughout the rest of this book, we'll focus on the code and not the development environment—but the details about creating the project, adding classes and resource files, and running and debugging are different. Our application is a simple BlackBerry application with a single screen that will display "Hello World". We'll walk through creating the workspace and project, creating and building out the necessary classes, and compiling and running on a simulator. Then, we'll add a few extra bits of polish, like a proper application name, version information, and an icon. Finally, you'll see how to build, sign, and run the application on an actual device.

We'll do all of this first using the stand-alone BlackBerry JDE and then using the BlackBerry JDE Plug-in for Eclipse. To avoid too much repetition, we'll discuss the code a bit more in-depth in the BlackBerry JDE section, so even if you plan on using the JDE Plug-in for Eclipse, you should read the section on the JDE first.

This is a quick-start chapter, so the goal is to gain basic proficiency with the development tools and a bit of understanding of the basics of a BlackBerry application without going too in depth. You'll probably have a lot of questions throughout this chapter, but the best way to proceed is to just go through step by step—things will become clearer as we explore details of application development later on.

There's a lot to do here, so let's get going.

Creating an Application with the BlackBerry JDE

The BlackBerry JDE is a fully integrated development environment that contains all the tools you need to develop, build, and test your application, on both a simulator and a device. Its editor, while quite usable, is not quite state-of-the-art, and if you're used to something like Visual Studio or Eclipse, you may find it a step backward. However, it makes up for this by supporting the widest range of features for BlackBerry development; there are times when only the JDE will do. And a lot of developers like it for its integrated nature and straightforward design and usage; you don't have to play with a lot of settings that might get in the way of developing your application.

If you don't have the JDE installed, please see Chapter 1 for information about where to get it and how to install it.

Creating the Workspace and Project

The BlackBerry JDE can have a single *workspace* loaded at any time. This workspace can contain any number of projects. Each project represents either a BlackBerry application, an alternate entry point to an application, a library, or a MIDlet. We'll discuss these all in the next chapter; for now, we'll just build a simple application.

Start by launching the JDE. If this is the first time you've launched it, you'll see the samples.jdw workspace already loaded. This contains an array of very useful sample applications from BlackBerry that show you how to use different parts of the BlackBerry API, and it's a great reference for application developers.

For now, we'll create our own workspace by selecting New Workspace from the File menu. Call the workspace HelloWorld, and select a directory to save it in, as shown in Figure 2-1.

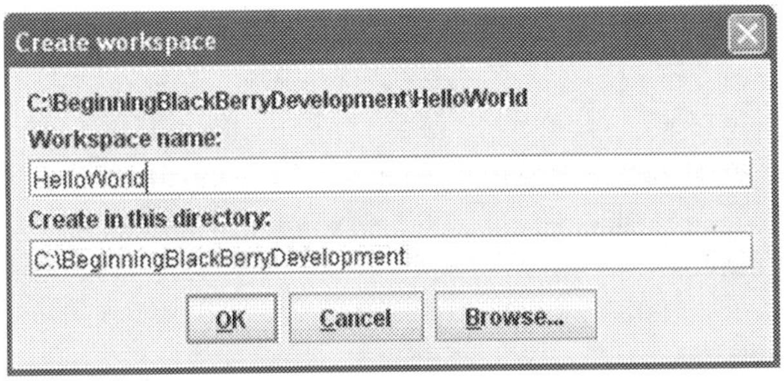

Figure 2-1. *The JDE Create Workspace dialog*

The JDE will create a file called HelloWorld.jdw in the directory that you specified

Next, create a BlackBerry application project in this workspace by right-clicking HelloWorld.jdw in the JDE and selecting "Create new Project in HelloWorld.jdw" from the pop-up menu, as shown in Figure 2-2.

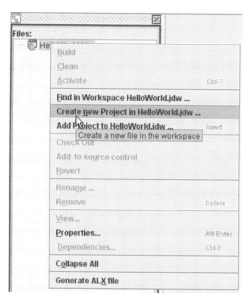

Figure 2-2. *Creating a new project in the JDE workspace*

We'll call this project HelloWorld as well, and leave the project in the same directory as the workspace, so just type **HelloWorld** in the "Project name" field as shown in Figure 2-3, and click OK.

Figure 2-3. *Creating the new project within the workspace*

There will now be a `HelloWorld.jdp` file in your directory. By default, this is already a BlackBerry application project (we'll talk about project types a little bit in the next chapter), so we don't have to do anything else.

Creating the Application Classes

Now, we'll create the Java classes that our Hello World application needs in much the same way as creating a project—right click the HelloWorld project, and select "Create new File in Project" as shown in Figure 2-4.

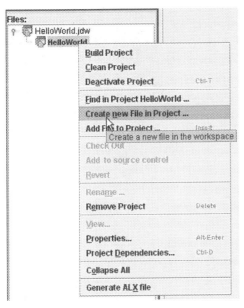

Figure 2-4. *Creating a new class in the JDE*

Call the new file HelloWorldApp (you can leave off the .java extension, as it will be added if you don't explicitly enter another file extension). It's also a very good idea to put your classes into packages. In the JDE, you can do this by specifying a subdirectory for the new class; the JDE will automatically map that to a package. We'll use com.beginningblackberry.helloworld as our package name, which maps to the directory com\beginningblackberry\helloworld. Add that to the end of the directory in the dialog box shown in Figure 2-5, and click OK.

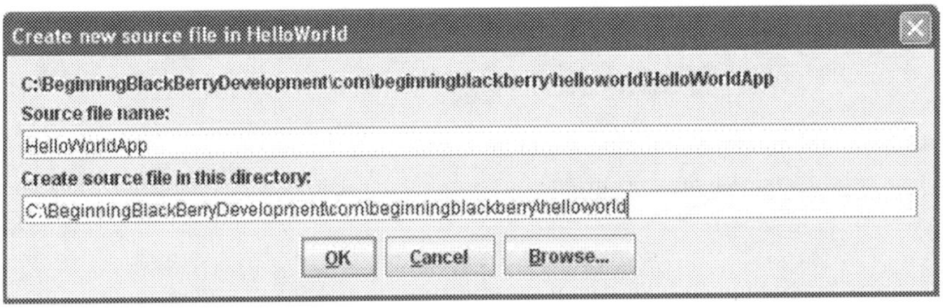

Create new source file in HelloWorld   ☒

C:\BeginningBlackBerryDevelopment\com\beginningblackberry\helloworld\HelloWorldApp
Source file name:

HelloWorldApp

Create source file in this directory:

C:\BeginningBlackBerryDevelopment\com\beginningblackberry\helloworld

OK   Cancel   Browse...

Figure 2-5. *Creating the main HelloWorldApp class in the JDE*

Now, the HelloWorldApp.java file will be created and opened by default in our workspace. The JDE helpfully fills in a basic class structure for us too, as shown in Figure 2-6.

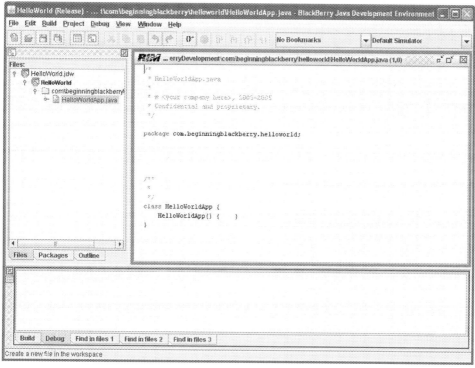

Figure 2-6. *HelloWorldApp.java*

We'll create one more class for our main screen and then start filling in details. Follow the same steps as before, and call the class HelloWorldMainScreen. Or, as a shortcut, you can right click the com/beginningblackberry/helloworld directory instead of the project name to have the JDE automatically fill in the package directory for you.

HelloWorldApp and HelloWorldMainScreen are the only classes we'll need for this application. The application project, as it appears in the JDE, is shown in Figure 2-7.

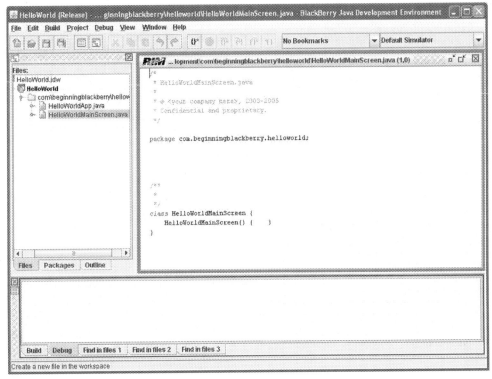

Figure 2-7. *Both classes for Hello World in the JDE*

The Main Application Class

The main application class will need to do three things:

- Create an instance of the application
- Create the main screen and push it onto the display stack
- Start the event dispatch thread

This is generally the pattern you'll follow for all your applications, unless you need to do something like automatically start when the BlackBerry device boots.

UiApplication

All applications that display a user interface (screens, menus, etc.) must subclass `net.rim.device.api.ui.UiApplication`. We'll do this by adding an import to the top of `HelloWorldApp.java` and making an appropriate change to the class definition (I've removed some of the automatically generated comments from the source to keep things shorter):

```
package com.beginningblackberry.helloworld;

import net.rim.device.api.ui.UiApplication;

class HelloWorldApp extends UiApplication {
    HelloWorldApp() {    }
}
```

> **NOTE:** We could have used import net.rim.device.api.ui.* to get the same result, but we imported the specific class instead. When you need to import a class, it's better to import that class specifically instead of the class's package. Doing so will improve application performance, and performance is very important on mobile devices.

Next, we'll fill in the constructor of HelloWorldApp. This will create the main screen and push it onto the display stack:

```
class HelloWorldApp extends UiApplication {
    HelloWorldApp() {
        HelloWorldMainScreen mainScreen = new HelloWorldMainScreen();
        pushScreen(mainScreen);
    }
}
```

Finally, we'll need a main method. This will be familiar to you if you're a Java SE, .NET, or C developer but is different from the Java ME/MIDP way of doing things. The main method acts as the entry point for our application and always has the same signature. You should only have one main method per application. The main method will create an instance of our application, and start the event dispatcher, which is the mechanism that does all the drawing to screen, and listens for all user interaction for our application.

```
class HelloWorldApp extends UiApplication {
    ...
    public static void main(String[] args) {
        HelloWorldApp app = new HelloWorldApp();
        app.enterEventDispatcher();
    }
}
```

The enterEventDispatcher method will never return as long as the application is running. Essentially, the thread that entered the main application becomes the event dispatch thread. We'll explore this in greater depth later, but for now, just remember that the method won't return during the application's normal life cycle.

Coding the Main Screen Class

If you tried to build the application at this point, you'd get a compile error, because we fudged something. The pushScreen call in HelloWorldApp's constructor requires a Screen object, which is a subclass of net.rim.device.api.ui.Screen, and HelloWorldMainScreen doesn't subclass that yet. Let's fix that now:

```
package com.beginningblackberry.helloworld;

import net.rim.device.api.ui.container.MainScreen;

class HelloWorldMainScreen extends MainScreen {
    HelloWorldMainScreen() {     }
}
```

We subclass MainScreen instead of Screen, because MainScreen gives us a couple of things automatically, namely a basic layout manager (to position our UI controls on the screen) and a default menu. Later, we'll want to handle some of that functionality ourselves, but for this application, the default behavior of MainScreen is just what we want.

You could run the application now, but you'd just get a blank screen (albeit with a menu containing the Close item). That's because we haven't added anything to our main screen yet. Let's do that and then build and run the application.

Adding Basic Fields

We'll deal with the user interface more in-depth later, but for now, here's a brief overview of how things work, so you're not walking totally blindfolded.

The BlackBerry User Interface API follows a Fields/Layout Managers/Screens model: Fields (the user interface controls like buttons and text boxes) are contained within layout managers, which arrange and draw them in specific positions. The managers themselves are contained within other managers, and ultimately a Screen class, which represents the visible display on the BlackBerry. If you've used Java's Abstract Window Toolkit (AWT), Swing, Windows Forms, or any number of other UI toolkits, these concepts will be familiar to you. In fact if you're an experienced Swing user, you'll find things very familiar.

For now, I'll gloss over some of the details, but basically, a MainScreen instance contains a single VerticalFieldManager instance, which arranges all fields that it contains, one below the other, in the order that they're added.

The BlackBerry API contains a useful variety of fields and managers already. For Hello World, we'll just need one—the LabelField, which displays (as you might expect) a text label. If you're interested in exploring a bit more, you can find most of the built-in fields in the net.rim.device.api.ui.component package and the built-in layout managers in net.rim.device.api.ui.container.

It's easier to show than explain, so here's what HelloWorldMainScreen looks like with the LabelField added:

```
package com.beginningblackberry.helloworld;

import net.rim.device.api.ui.container.MainScreen;
import net.rim.device.api.ui.component.LabelField;
```

```
class HelloWorldMainScreen extends MainScreen {
    HelloWorldMainScreen() {
        LabelField labelField = new LabelField("Hello World");
        add(labelField);
    }
}
```

Now, the application's finished! Let's take a look at it in action in the simulator.

Running the Simulator

Running an application in the simulator is very easy. Remember when we talked about how easy setup is with the JDE? From the Debug menu, click Go—that's it. The JDE will automatically build your project (hopefully, you don't have any build errors) and deploy it to the simulator, and the default simulator for your version of the JDE will start. We used the JDE version 4.2.1, which has the BlackBerry 8800 as its default simulator, so we get a window that looks like this the one shown in Figure 2-8.

Figure 2-8. *The default JDE version 4.2.1 simulator is the BlackBerry 8800.*

Your application won't be started by default, so you'll have to navigate to it and start it. There are two things to remember with the simulator:

- Unless you're using the JDE version 4.7 with the BlackBerry Storm simulator, you can't click the screen—well, you can, but it won't do anything, as most BlackBerry devices don't have touch screens.

▓ The trackball registers up, down, left, and right movements; it basically like the arrow keys on your keyboard. In fact, the easiest way to operate the trackball in the simulator is to use the arrow keys on your PC's keyboard.

For most devices, to run the application in the simulator, you can follow these instructions:

1. Navigate down to the Applications icon (the bottom one on the list), and press Enter on your keyboard (see Figure 2-9).

Figure 2-9. *The Applications icon on the simulator*

2. Navigate to the HelloWorld icon (see Figure 2-10), and press Enter.

Figure 2-10. *The HelloWorld Icon on the simulator*

3. The application will start: `HelloWorldMainScreen` will display our `LabelField`, which says Hello World as shown in Figure 2-11.

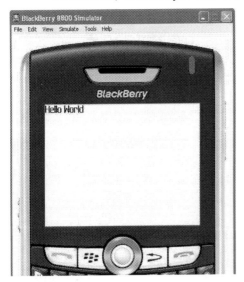

Figure 2-11. *Hello world!*

This application is not the most exciting, certainly, but it's a real, fully functional application. It has a menu with a Close menu item (you can open the menu by clicking the BlackBerry key to the left of the trackball), and you can start and exit it, and with a tiny bit of work, you'll be able to put it onto a real device. The first thing we'll need to do is build and sign our application.

Building and Signing Your Application

Building on the JDE is as simple as clicking Build from the Build menu.

The Hello World application is simple enough that you don't need to sign it to run on a device, but it's a good idea to get used to signing your applications for when you will need it. If you don't have your code signing keys yet, you can skip the rest of this section.

After you've built your application, select Request Signatures from the Build menu. Notice that all signatures are listed as optional (See Figure 2-12). We don't need to sign, but it won't hurt, so click the Request button, and enter your password. You'll see a progress dialog and, if all goes well, messages letting you know that your application has been signed.

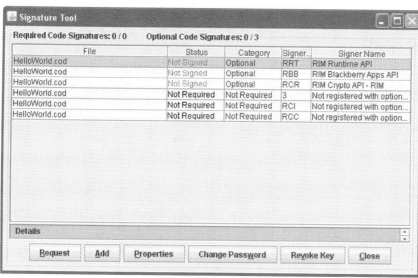

Figure 2-12. *Requesting signatures for Hello World*

Building with Different JDE Versions

If you want to build with different versions of the JDE, you'll have to reload your workspace under each version of the JDE you want to use.

Generally, building with the earliest version that supports all the features that you need is a good idea. This gives your application compatibility with the widest range of BlackBerry devices.

You may need to build and run under a later version if you want to test with a simulator (such as the touch screen BlackBerry Storm) that's only available for certain versions of the JDE. Also, if you want to use a specific API, you'll obviously need to use the appropriate version of the JDE; JDE versions that APIs appear in are usually specified in the BlackBerry API Javadocs.

Loading Hello World onto a Device

You can load a BlackBerry application onto a device in several ways. For now, to avoid discussion of different descriptor files, we'll use a developer tool called JavaLoader.

JavaLoader is a command-line tool, meaning you have to run it from the Windows command prompt. Start a command prompt window, and navigate to your working directory. Then, make sure your BlackBerry is plugged into a USB port on your computer before typing the following:

```
<Path to JDE bin> \JavaLoader.exe -u load HelloWorld.cod
```

Replace <Path to JDE bin> with the path to the bin directory under your JDE installation, usually C:\Program Files\Research In Motion\BlackBerry JDE 4.2.1\bin\.

Your application should load on to your device almost instantly, and you'll be ready to show off Hello World to your friends!

Using the Debugger

The simulator and JDE debugger are as powerful a combination as you'd expect from any modern development environment. You can simulate different network coverage, battery levels, and other device configurations, as well as events like phone calls through the Simulate menu. You can also set a breakpoint and step through your code at any point.

Of course, no simulator is a 100 percent perfect representation of the real thing, so the debugger also lets you connect to your application running on a real BlackBerry device through a USB connection.

Changing Simulators and Settings

Your choice of simulators is limited to those that came with the version of the JDE you're using and any others you've downloaded and installed (see Chapter 1). To select a simulator other than the default, select Preferences from the Edit menu, and click the Simulator tab (see Figure 2-13).

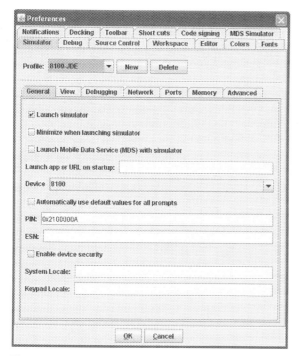

Figure 2-13. *The Simulator tab in the JDE's Preferences window*

On the Simulator tab, you can choose a specific simulator to run and modify quite a few other useful parameters, for example:

- *PIN*: This is often used as a unique device ID for a client-server application.

- *Launch Mobile Data Service (MDS) with simulator*: This is required for simulating most BlackBerry networking applications. We'll use and discuss this in Chapter 7.

Setting Breakpoints

Setting a breakpoint is easy. Just right-click somewhere in your source file, and select Set Breakpoint At Cursor (or press F9 to set a breakpoint at the line the cursor is currently on). A breakpoint will cause your application to pause and open the debug view when that line is reached. From that point, you can step through your code line-by-line to look at the values of variables, the call stack, and other information.

Let's try this with Hello World now. Open HelloWorldMainScreen.java in the editor and move the cursor to the first line in the constructor, as shown in Figure 2-14.

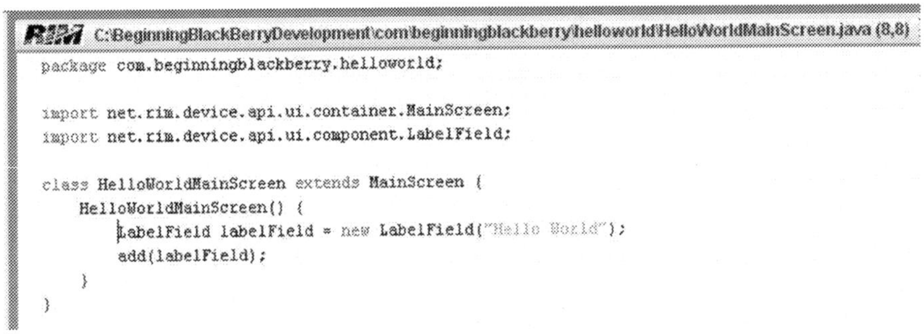

```
RIM   C:\BeginningBlackBerryDevelopment\com\beginningblackberry\helloworld\HelloWorldMainScreen.java (8,8)
package com.beginningblackberry.helloworld;

import net.rim.device.api.ui.container.MainScreen;
import net.rim.device.api.ui.component.LabelField;

class HelloWorldMainScreen extends MainScreen {
    HelloWorldMainScreen() {
        LabelField labelField = new LabelField("Hello World");
        add(labelField);
    }
}
```

Figure 2-14. *Move the cursor to the first line of the HelloWorldMainScreen constructor.*

Right-click, and add a breakpoint. You'll see a red ball indicating the breakpoint, as shown in Figure 2-15.

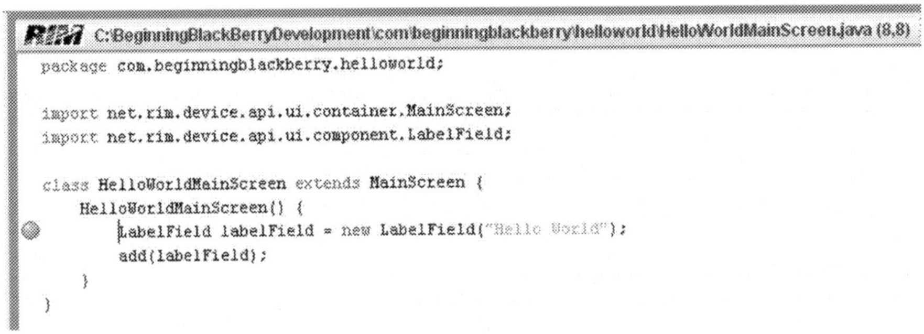

```
RIM   C:\BeginningBlackBerryDevelopment\com\beginningblackberry\helloworld\HelloWorldMainScreen.java (8,8)
package com.beginningblackberry.helloworld;

import net.rim.device.api.ui.container.MainScreen;
import net.rim.device.api.ui.component.LabelField;

class HelloWorldMainScreen extends MainScreen {
    HelloWorldMainScreen() {
        LabelField labelField = new LabelField("Hello World");
        add(labelField);
    }
}
```

Figure 2-15. *A breakpoint is indicated by the circle to the left of the LabelField initialization.*

Now, start the simulator if it isn't still running, and start the application. Since this breakpoint is in a constructor, the debugger should come up right away (see Figure 2-16). The JDE window will have a few new panels available, including the Calling Method panel. It displays that call stack and shows that we're in the HelloWorldMainScreen constructor, which was called from the HelloWorldApp constructor, which was called from the main method in HelloWorldApp.

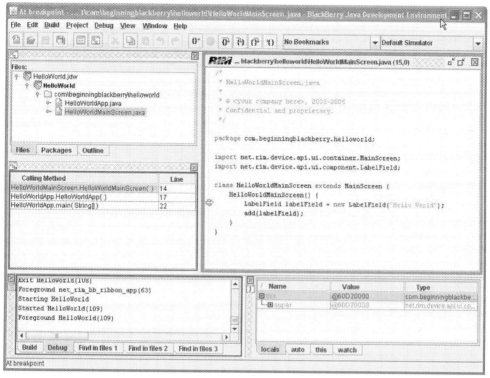

Figure 2-16. *Execution stopped at a breakpoint with the JDE. The call stack is visible in the middle-left panel and the variables in the bottom-right one.*

In the bottom-right panel is a list of variables that are currently in scope. If we step to the next line (using F10 or Debug ➤ Step Over), labelField will appear in that list.

Additional information and functionality, such as profiling, is available from the View menu.

Debugging on a BlackBerry Device

Debugging on a device lets you test things that are difficult or impossible with the simulator like specific network conditions and memory and speed constraints. The debugger lets you set breakpoints that will cause the device to suspend execution, as well as allowing you to see the output of System.out.println statements in your application.

To debug your application on a device, you must have your device connected to your computer via USB cable. Also, the BlackBerry Desktop Manager should *not* be running; it will cause connection problems with the debugger.

With your BlackBerry device plugged in and the application loaded (but not running), click the Debug menu, and select Attach To. Your device's PIN should appear in the menu as in Figure 2-17. Click it, and after a few seconds for the debugger to attach (messages will appear on the device's screen), you'll be able to do everything you can with a simulator.

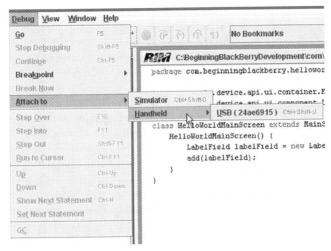

Figure 2-17. *Attaching the debugger to a real device*

Now, if you've kept the same breakpoint from the "Setting Breakpoints" section, when you launch the application the JDE will pop up in the same view with an arrow pointing to the breakpoint at the same line.

Creating an Application with the BlackBerry JDE Plug-in for Eclipse

The JDE Plug-in for Eclipse hasn't been around as long as the stand-alone JDE and, until fairly recently, wasn't as well supported, so there are still a few things that may not work 100 percent of the time. Also, the JDE Plug-in supports only JDE version 4.2.1 and later. Neither of these limitations is a concern for the majority of projects: the flakier parts are fairly obscure and don't affect the final application, and version 4.2.1 is pretty much the minimum that most commercial applications should realistically support. The benefit is the richness of the Eclipse environment—mainly Eclipse's editor, which has many more features than the one included with the JDE. For what it's worth, I have used earlier versions of the JDE Plug-in for Eclipse to create many professional BlackBerry applications, and even with its quirks, I would recommend it to any developer.

We'll walk through creating the same Hello World application with the JDE Plug-in for Eclipse, but I'll skimp a bit on explanations of the code this time, so if you don't understand something about the structure of the program itself, refer to the previous sections.

If you haven't installed the JDE Plug-in for Eclipse, refer to Chapter 1 for instructions about where to get it and how to install it.

Creating the Project

With Eclipse, workspace creation is implicit, and the JDE Plug-in uses the same concept of workspace as Eclipse itself does. When you start Eclipse, you're asked for a workspace location, which can be any directory. Select (or create) an appropriate one and click OK, as shown in Figure 2-18.

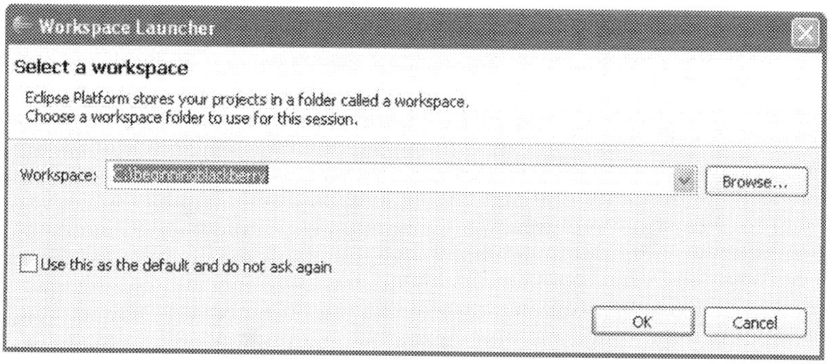

Figure 2-18. *Creating a new workspace in Eclipse*

If this is the first time you've opened this workspace, you'll see Eclipse's new workspace Welcome screen (see Figure 2-19). There are useful things here, but for this tutorial, just click "Go to the workbench".

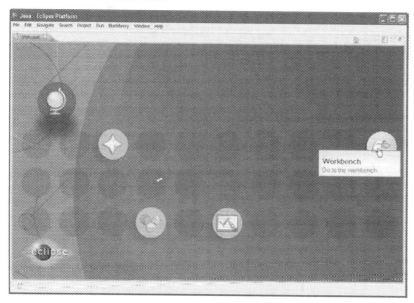

Figure 2-19. *The Eclipse new workspace Welcome page*

To create a new BlackBerry project, click the File menu, and choose New ➤ Project.

In the New Project dialog, select BlackBerry Project from the BlackBerry folder, as shown in Figure 2-20.

Figure 2-20. *The Eclipse New Project dialog*

Click Next; name your project HelloWorld, and click Finish. Your Eclipse workspace should contain a single project in the Package Explorer on the left-hand side. When expanded, the package should contain a folder named src, which is where all our source files will reside, and a reference to NET_RIM_BLACKBERRY, which is the BlackBerry runtime library containing the BlackBerry API, as shown in Figure 2-21.

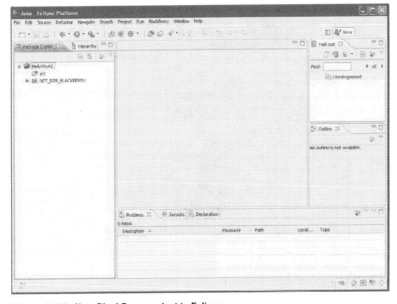

Figure 2-21. *New BlackBerry project in Eclipse*

Creating the Application Classes

Here's where the power of Eclipse will start to become apparent. We'll create the same two classes for our project as we did with the JDE, but Eclipse will let us generate a lot more of the code automatically.

Creating the Main Application Class

Right-click the HelloWorld project icon in the Package Explorer, and from the pop-up menu, select New ➤ Class. In the dialog, type the following values:

- *Package*: com.beginningblackberry
- *Name*: HelloWorldApp
- *Superclass*: net.rim.device.api.ui.UiApplication

> **NOTE:** A handy shortcut throughout Eclipse, both in the New Java Class dialog and in the code editor, is to type part of the class name and then press Ctrl+space to get a list of class suggestions. For example, to automatically get the class name net.rim.device.api.ui.UiApplication in the Superclass field of the New Java Class dialog, type **UiApp** and press Ctrl+space. Eclipse will look for possible completions in the RIM API and in any classes you've created in your workspace. It also works for other Java constructs, such as method names.

Under "Which method stubs would you like to create?" , make sure the first two check boxes for generating a main method and constructors are checked (the third box can be checked or not, there are no abstract methods in UiApplication, so it won't make a difference). Everything else can be left at the default (see Figure 2-22).

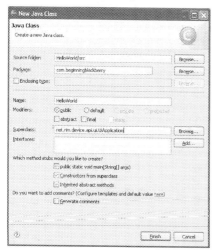

Figure 2-22. *Creating the main application class with Eclipse*

You'll get the following source code:

```
package com.beginningblackberry;

import net.rim.device.api.ui.UiApplication;

public class HelloWorldApp extends UiApplication {

    public HelloWorldApp() {
        // TODO Auto-generated constructor stub
    }

    /**
     * @param args
     */
    public static void main(String[] args) {
        // TODO Auto-generated method stub

    }

}
```

There are even TODO markers where we have to write our logic. We'll do that, but first, let's create the main screen class.

Creating the Main Screen Class

Click New ➤ Class again (or if you right-click the package in the tree view and select New ➤ Class, you won't have to reenter the package name). Fill in the following values:

- *Package*: com.beginningblackberry
- *Name*: HelloWorldMainScreen
- *Superclass*: net.rim.device.api.ui.container.MainScreen (or type **MainS**, and press Ctrl+space)

Leave all other values as default, and click Finish to create the following source code:

```
package com.beginningblackberry;

import net.rim.device.api.ui.container.MainScreen;

public class HelloWorldMainScreen extends MainScreen {

}
```

Filling in the Hello World Classes

Now, we'll fill in the logic for both of our classes as in the previous sections (the code is repeated here for your convenience).

First, add the code for HelloWorldApp.java:

```
package com.beginningblackberry;
```

```
import net.rim.device.api.ui.UiApplication;

public class HelloWorldApp extends UiApplication {

    public HelloWorldApp() {
        HelloWorldMainScreen mainScreen = new HelloWorldMainScreen();
        pushScreen(mainScreen);
    }

    /**
     * @param args
     */
    public static void main(String[] args) {
        HelloWorldApp app = new HelloWorldApp();
        app.enterEventDispatcher();
    }

}
```

Then, add the following code for HelloWorldMainScreen.java:

```
package com.beginningblackberry;

import net.rim.device.api.ui.component.LabelField;
import net.rim.device.api.ui.container.MainScreen;

public class HelloWorldMainScreen extends MainScreen {
    public HelloWorldMainScreen() {
        LabelField labelField = new LabelField("Hello World");
        add(labelField);
    }
}
```

Running the Simulator

As with the JDE, the application is automatically built and deployed when we launch the simulator (in fact, with Eclipse, the Java code is compiled whenever you make any change, which makes spotting errors easy). Running the simulator involves an extra step or two, because you have to create a debug configuration. The advantage of this is that you can create multiple device configurations for different simulators and quickly select whichever one you need.

Click the arrow next to the debug icon in the Eclipse toolbar, and select Debug Configurations, as shown in Figure 2-23.

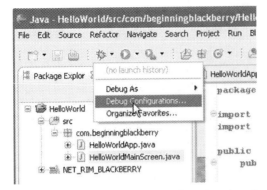

Figure 2-23. *The Eclipse debug configurations drop-down*

The Debug Configurations dialog (see Figure 2-24) lets you set up different configurations, which may be different simulators or actual devices. Each configuration can have different debug parameters, and as you develop applications, you'll likely end up with a few different configurations for debugging different operating system versions, screen sizes, and so on. Feel free to explore these options at any time.

For now, select the BlackBerry Simulator icon on the left side, and click the New button on the toolbar in the dialog window that's shown in Figure 2-23.

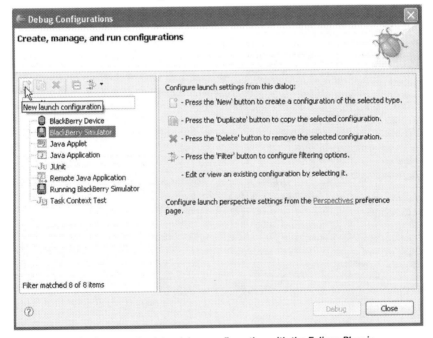

Figure 2-24. *Setting up a simulator debug configuration with the Eclipse Plug-in*

We'll keep all the defaults, so just click the Debug button at the bottom of the dialog shown in Figure 2-25, and the simulator will launch with your application deployed. From this point on, you can access your debug configuration directly from the Debug drop-down menu in the main Eclipse toolbar by clicking the downward-facing arrow next to the debug icon.

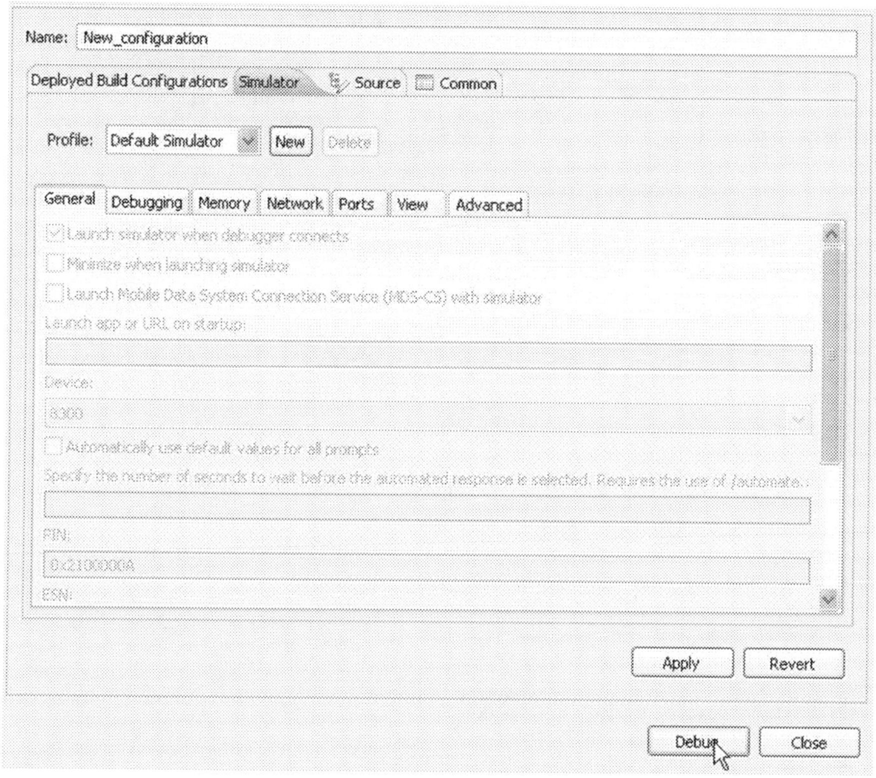

Figure 2-25. *The default values for a new debug configuration*

Using Breakpoints and the Debug Perspective

A breakpoint can be set for a line from the Run menu, using Toggle Breakpoint.

When the application stops at a breakpoint, you'll be prompted to show the Eclipse Debug perspective. The Debug perspective gives you the same information as the JDE, arranged slightly differently (see Figure 2-26).

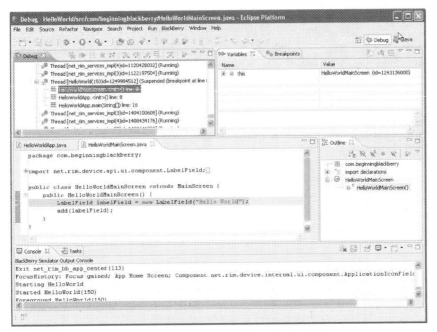

Figure 2-26. *The Eclipse Debug perspective, stopped at a breakpoint.*

All the same functionality that was available in the JDE is available here, using Eclipse's keyboard shortcuts and menus, of course. More debugging information is available from the Window menu, under Show View.

Building and Signing Your Application

The concepts are the same for building and signing with the JDE Plug-in for Eclipse as with the JDE. To build your application, open the Project menu, and click Build Active BlackBerry Configuration.

To sign the application, open the BlackBerry menu, and select Request Signatures. The same dialog will appear as you saw with the JDE.

Building with Different JDE Versions

Building with different versions of the JDE using the JDE Plug-in is accomplished by changing your workspace configuration. By default, the JDE Plug-in comes with a single version of the JDE; you must download others as outlined in Chapter 1.

The easiest way to access your JDE configuration is by clicking Configure BlackBerry Workspace from the BlackBerry menu. You'll be presented with the Eclipse Preferences window, opened to the BlackBerry JDE section.

This window is worth exploring a bit on your own time, but for now, click the Installed Components item in the left-hand tree view (see Figure 2-27).

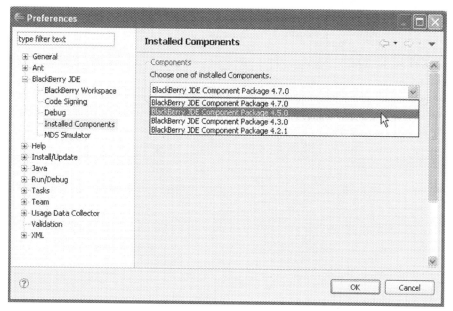

Figure 2-27. *Changing JDE Versions in Eclipse*

You'll see a list of all of your installed JDE versions. Select one, and click OK. You'll be prompted to rebuild your workspace with the new JDE version.

> **NOTE:** You can only run debug configurations corresponding to your currently selected JDE version. Others will still show up in the debug drop-down, however. Selecting an incompatible one won't cause any harm but will result in an error dialog.

Debugging on a Device

Like the JDE, the JDE Plug-in allows you to debug code on a real device. This requires the creation of a new debug configuration. From the Debug toolbar menu, select Debug Configurations, and create a new BlackBerry Device configuration by highlighting that icon and clicking the New button, as shown in Figure 2-28).

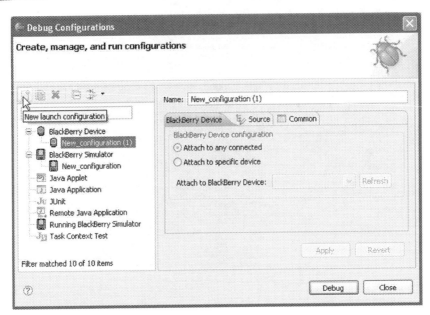

Figure 2-28. *Setting up for on-device debugging using the Eclipse Plug-in*

Polishing the Application

Now that we've created and run our first application in the JDE or Eclipse (or both), we'll finish off by adding a few bits of polish: the application icon and a slightly friendlier name.

Setting the Title in Project Properties

The application title and version are both accessed through the project properties dialog, which is in almost the same place in both development environments. In the JDE, it's accessed by right-clicking the project and selecting Properties. In Eclipse, it's accessed by right-clicking the name of the project in the left-hand pane, selecting Properties and clicking BlackBerry Project Properties in the list on the left side (the other items in the list are properties that apply to all types of Eclipse projects, which are outside the scope of this book).

If you don't specify an application title, the BlackBerry will use your project name as the title of the application on the home screen. In our case, we want a space between Hello and World and add an exclamation point to make it more exciting, so type **Hello World!** in the Title field (Figure 2-29 shows the JDE project properties dialog).

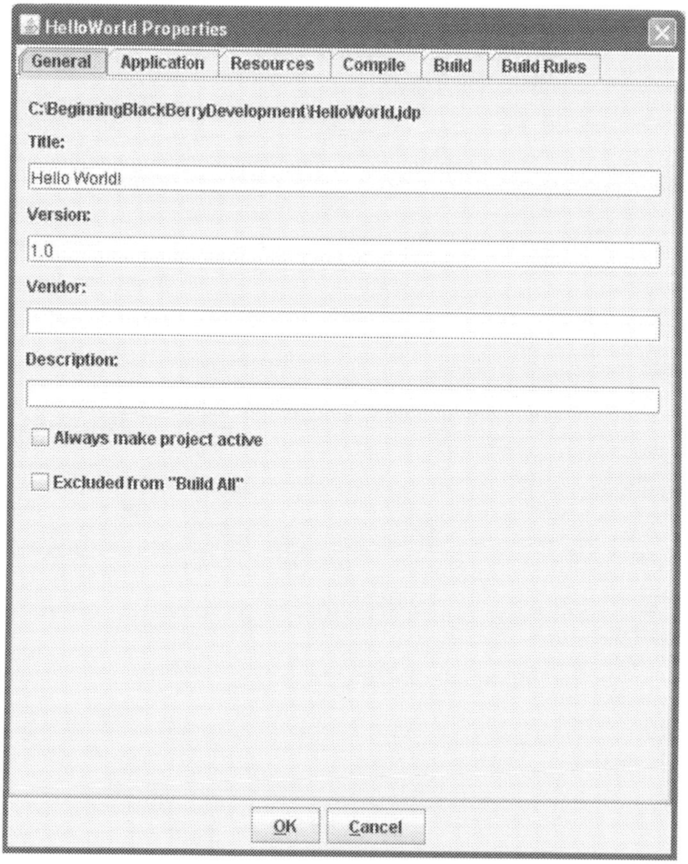

Figure 2-29. *The properties dialog for the HelloWorld project*

Creating an Icon

A BlackBerry icon should be a PNG image. Because there are different screen resolutions, the image size will depend on the devices you want to support, though 48 × 48 pixels is reasonable for most devices (many older ones will scale it down). For more information about ideal icon sizes for different devices you can refer to the BlackBerry UI Guidelines. The easiest way to find them is to search the BlackBerry Developer Zone (see Chapter 1) for "UI Guidelines." You can download the icon file I used from the book's page of the Apress website.

Adding an Icon with the JDE

Using the JDE, you must add the icon's image file to the project before using it as your application icon. Save the file to a directory under your project. Then from the Project menu, select Add File to Project, and browse for your icon file. Your workspace should now list icon.png on the left side (see Figure 2-30).

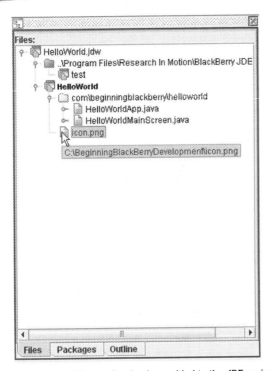

Figure 2-30. *The application icon added to the JDE project*

Now, right-click the icon, and select Properties. Select the Use As Application Icon check box in the File Properties dialog (see Figure 2-31).

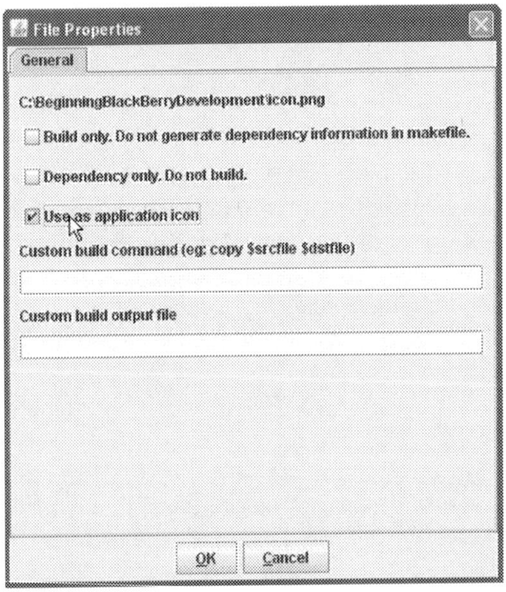

Figure 2-31. *Setting icon.png to be used as the applicaton's icon*

Adding an Icon with the JDE Plug-in for Eclipse

The JDE Plug-in doesn't require you to add the icon to the workspace before making it the application icon. In fact, the icon's image file doesn't even have to be in the project directory (though storing it with the project is highly recommended, as it makes managing everything easier). Right-click your project, and select Properties to open the project properties, dialog. Then, click BlackBerry Project Properties, followed by the Resources tab, and click the Add button under "Icon files" (see Figure 2-32). Then browse for your icon.

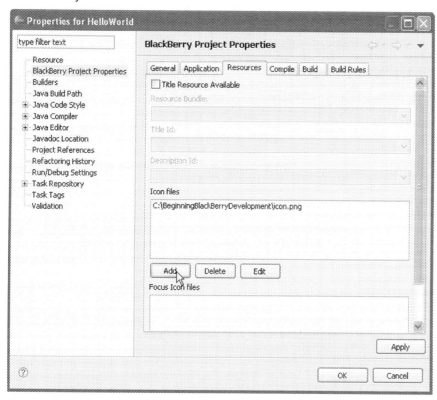

Figure 2-32. *Adding the Hello World application icon in Eclipse*

Seeing It All in Action

Now, go ahead and run the simulator again. Our fancy new icon and more user-friendly name will be displayed on the home screen, just like in Figure 2-33!

Figure 2-33. *The shiny new Hello World! name and icon*

Summary

Congratulations! You've successfully built your first BlackBerry application. You've learned how to run and debug it in the simulator and how to load and debug it on a real BlackBerry device. That's a good start, but obviously, we haven't even scratched the surface of the rich BlackBerry API, so there's a lot still to learn. In the next chapter, we'll briefly discuss and consolidate some of the concepts that you learned here and set the stage for our deeper exploration of the BlackBerry API.

Chapter 3

What Makes a BlackBerry Application?

You should now be familiar with the basics of building a BlackBerry application using the stand-alone JDE or the JDE Plug-in for Eclipse. Before really diving into what the BlackBerry API can do, we'll digress briefly to discuss a few concepts that apply to BlackBerry application development. If you're eager to get coding, you can skip to the next chapter, but I recommend you at least skim over this one first, so you know what's discussed here and can refer to it later as necessary. We'll cover some fundamental things that will be used heavily in the next couple of chapters, including the user interface threading model and the BlackBerry API Javadocs. We'll also cover a few things that are useful to know in many types of applications, like application life cycle, foreground and background applications, and the different types of BlackBerry projects you can create using the development environment.

Javadocs

The BlackBerry development environment comes with API documentation in the Javadoc format (See Figure 3-1). Javadocs should be familiar to Java developers; basically, these form a set of HTML files for each class in the API, detailing all the methods and other properties of each class. You'll find yourself referring to the Javadocs frequently, so it's good to know where to find them. They're also a great way to explore the API and get an idea of what's possible.

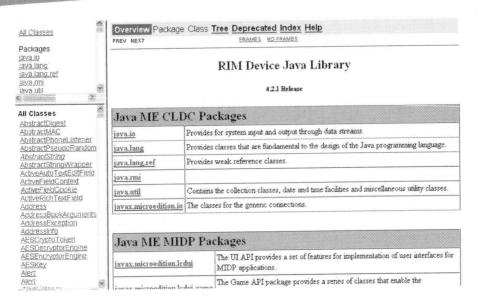

Figure 3-1. *The BlackBerry API Javadocs*

If you've installed the stand-alone JDE, you can find the Javadocs through the Windows Start menu at Research In Motion ➤ BlackBerry JDE 4.2.1 ➤ API JavaDoc Reference (or a similar place for different versions of the JDE).

With the JDE Plug-in for Eclipse, the Javadocs are located on the filesystem under the Eclipse installation directory. For example, the 4.2.1 component pack is located here: `eclipse\plugins\net.rim.eide.componentpack4.2.1_4.2.1.17\components\docs\api\index.html`.

You can also see the Javadoc for any class or method in the Eclipse editor by hovering the mouse pointer over the class or method name for a few seconds as in Figure 3-2.

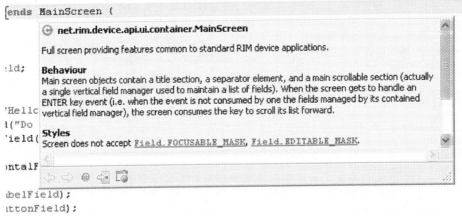

Figure 3-2. *Viewing the Javadoc for MainScreen class in Eclipse by hovering the mouse pointer*

The BlackBerry Application Life Cycle

BlackBerry applications behave very much like ordinary desktop applications. If you've had experience with C, C++, or Java on the desktop, some of the ideas in the previous chapter probably seemed very familiar to you. Specifically, the main method for a BlackBerry application is identical to the main method for a Java SE application (which is very similar to C's).

While there are exceptions for specific needs, almost all BlackBerry applications will follow the same life cycle. In this book, all of our applications will fundamentally look like the Hello World application we created in the last chapter.

Starting the Application

An application is generally started in one of three ways:

- The user clicks the application's icon on the BlackBerry home screen.

- The application is an automatically starting application and runs when the device is turned on or after it reboots.

- The application is run by another application.

In all cases, the main method is the first entry point for your application. The BlackBerry device will create a process, which will call that method. Whenever the main method exits, the process is terminated and your application exits. This means that if you want your application to do anything, you'd better do it in that main method.

The main method takes an array of java.lang.String objects as parameters. For the most part, this array is empty, but parameters can be passed in if you define them in the project properties or if they're passed by another process that is starting your application.

Creating the Application

All BlackBerry applications that want to present a user interface to the user must extend UiApplication. You can only create one instance of UiApplication for any application process; the BlackBerry runtime will throw an exception if you try to instantiate a second one.

Even applications with no user interface must extend net.rim.device.api.system.Application, but those types of applications are outside the scope of this book.

You can always access your application instance using the static method UiApplication.getUiApplication(). This actually returns an instance of your application class, so from anywhere in Hello World, the following is allowed:

```
HelloWorldApp helloWorld = (HelloWorldApp)UiApplication.getUiApplication();
```

Invoking the Event Thread

The event thread is started for you by the BlackBerry operating system, but it doesn't start processing events and drawing the UI until you explicitly tell it to. You do this with the UiApplication.enterEventDispatcher() call that you saw in the last chapter. Once this method is called, the thread that entered into the main method passes from your direct control and takes up the task of listening for user interface input and drawing the user interface to the screen. You'll still get a chance to do work on the thread, but for the most part, its activities are scheduled by the BlackBerry operating system. enterEventDispatcher won't return for the entire life cycle of your application, so if there's anything your main thread must do before calling this (for example, some types of initialization) you have only one chance.

Processing Events

The application responds to keyboard input, trackball, or touch screen movements and clicks and to other events like system messages.

Exiting the Application

Generally, a BlackBerry application exits when the last screen is removed from the display stack (by closing it). You may have noticed the System.exit() method, which will exit the application, but it's recommended to avoid this and properly clean up the application on exiting by closing all screens instead. When the application exits, all application state will be cleaned up, and the next time the user clicks the application icon the main method will be called again with a new process.

Threading and the Event Thread

The BlackBerry UI API is single-threaded. This means that all UI updates and events are handled by the same thread—or more precisely, must be done while holding the event lock, which most of the time is held by the UI thread. It also has a couple of implications for BlackBerry applications: other threads can't directly access the UI without explicitly acquiring the event lock (an exception will be thrown if you try), and if you perform an operation on the event thread that takes a long time, the entire user interface will pause while that operation is taking place.

The message to take away from all this is to get comfortable with using at least one or two other threads in your applications.

NOTE: We're not going to be doing heavy concurrency in this book, so if you're understand what a thread is and how to create and start one, you'll be fine. However, if you're not comfortable with the idea of threading at all, or have never used threads in your programming, I recommend you take a look at the Java SE threading API.

Knowing When Your Application Is on the Event Thread

You can always tell if your code is being executed by the event thread by calling UiApplication.isEventDispatchThread(). Generally though, you shouldn't need to invoke this. A good rule of thumb for determining if you're on the event thread is: If your code was invoked more or less directly from the run method of a Thread that you created, you're not on the event thread. If the code was invoked by the system in response to user input (for example, a menu item or a button click), you're on the event thread.

Updating the UI from Other Threads

Of course, many times, you want an event in another thread to be reflected in the UI, for example, to show progress of a long network activity like a file download. To do that, there are a couple of methods. The first is to use UiApplication.invokeLater or UiApplication.invokeAndWait to tell the UI thread to run some code on the event thread at the next available opportunity. The second method is to acquire the UI event lock by synchronizing on the object returned by UiApplication.getEventLock(). We'll explore the first method by modifying Hello World to start a thread that adds a message to the main screen's Label field every 5 seconds.

NOTE: Both invokeLater and invokeAndWait do the same thing—queue an instance of java.lang.Runnable to be executed on the event thread. The difference is that invokeLater returns immediately, while invokeAndWait doesn't return until the run method of your Runnable has finished executing and, therefore, blocks the thread that calls it

First, let's change labelField to be a member variable instead of a variable local to the constructor, and add a method to append text to it:

```
public class HelloWorldMainScreen extends MainScreen {

    private LabelField labelField;

    public HelloWorldMainScreen() {
        labelField = new LabelField("Hello World");
        add(labelField);
    }
```

```
        public void appendLabelText(String text) {
            labelField.setText(labelField.getText() + "\n" + text);
        }

    }
```

Because appendLabelText calls LabelField.setText, the call can only be made from the event thread. If you attempt to call this method directly from another thread, an exception will be thrown.

Now, we'll define the thread class that will actually do the updating. It will loop from 1 to 10. In each iteration, it will wait 5 seconds and then add some text to the LabelField. Create a new class called MainScreenUpdaterThread that extends java.lang.Thread. The full source code follows:

```
package com.beginningblackberry;

import net.rim.device.api.ui.UiApplication;

public class MainScreenUpdaterThread extends Thread {
    HelloWorldMainScreen mainScreen;

    public MainScreenUpdaterThread(HelloWorldMainScreen mainScreen) {
        this.mainScreen = mainScreen;
    }

    public void run() {
        for (int i = 0; i < 10; i++) {

            try {
                Thread.sleep(5000);
            } catch (InterruptedException ex) {

            }
            // Queue a new task on the event thread
            UiApplication.getUiApplication().invokeLater(new Runnable() {
                public void run() {
                    mainScreen.appendLabelText("Update");
                }

            });

        }
    }
}
```

To actually update the UI, we're using an anonymous inner class, which is a class that we define at the point where we instantiate it. Our anonymous inner class calls the one method that needs to be called on the event thread—appendLabelText (which calls LabelField.setText).

We'll start our thread in the HelloWorldMainScreen constructor as follows:

```
    public HelloWorldMainScreen() {
        labelField = new LabelField("Hello World");
        add(labelField);
```

```
MainScreenUpdaterThread thread = new MainScreenUpdaterThread(this);
thread.start();
}
```

Finally, running this application will produce the output shown in Figure 3-3.

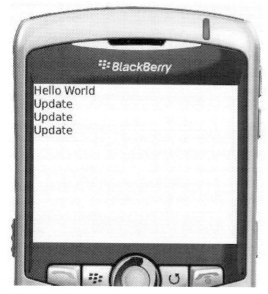

Figure 3-3. *A few updates from our thread*

Using the Event Lock

What about the second method of updating the UI from another thread? With a simple modification to MainScreenUpdaterThread we can do that too. Change the run method of MainScreenUpdaterThread to the following:

```
public void run() {
    for (int i = 0; i < 10; i++) {
        try {
            Thread.sleep(5000);
        } catch (InterruptedException ex) {

        }
        // Ensure we have the event lock
        synchronized(UiApplication.getEventLock()) {
            mainScreen.appendLabelText("Update");
        }
    }
}
```

The application should run exactly the same way as in the previous example.

This example application is admittedly a bit contrived, but it's important to understand the concept of updating the UI from a different thread, as this concept will be applied throughout most BlackBerry applications you create.

Running Background Applications

While an application, by default, will exit when the last screen is closed, you can override this behavior to send an application to the background instead, meaning that the UI will not be displayed, but the application will continue to run as the user performs other tasks. Running applications in the background is useful in the following situations:

- You want your application to periodically check for changes on the device or for events. For example, the BlackBerry Messages application always runs to check for incoming mail.

- You want to periodically download new information from the network. Several weather and stock applications use this approach.

- You need to maintain a connection to an external server. An instant messaging application might need to maintain a connection to the messaging server.

Detecting Backgrounding or Foregrounding

An application can be sent to the background if a user when presses the red phone key or explicitly switches tasks. You can detect this background status by overriding the UiApplication.deactivate method. Similarly, you can detect your application coming back into the foreground by overriding UiApplication.activate.

Let's modify HelloWorldApp to display a message when Hello World goes to the background or comes to the foreground:

```
public class HelloWorldApp extends UiApplication {

    private HelloWorldMainScreen mainScreen;

    public HelloWorldApp() {
        mainScreen = new HelloWorldMainScreen();
        pushScreen(mainScreen);
    }

    public void deactivate() {
        mainScreen.appendLabelText("Went to background");
    }

    public void activate() {
        mainScreen.appendLabelText("Came to foreground");
    }

    /**
     * @param args
     */
    public static void main(String[] args) {
        HelloWorldApp app = new HelloWorldApp();
        app.enterEventDispatcher();
    }

}
```

When you run this application, you'll immediately see a "Came to foreground" message. The message is displayed because of the initial activation of the application. Press the red button, and then select the icon a few times to send the application back and forth from foreground to background. You'll see something like Figure 3-4.

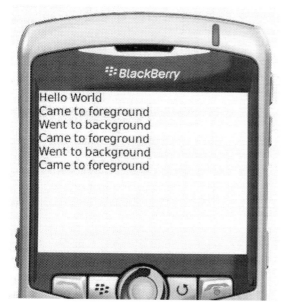

Figure 3-4. *Hello World after going between the background and foreground a few times.*

Sending Your Application to the Background

You can send your application to the background using the UiApplication.requestBackground() method. To make Hello World go to the background rather than exit when the user closes the main screen, let's override Screen.close() in HelloWorldMainScreen:

```
public class HelloWorldMainScreen extends MainScreen {
    //...

    public void close() {
        UiApplication.getUiApplication().requestBackground();
    }
}
```

Now, pressing the escape key or selecting Close from Hello World will actually send the application to the background. You can test that this produces the same messages as in the example shown in Figure 3-4.

Understanding the Types of Projects

I mentioned this topic earlier, but it deserves a little more discussion now. Using the JDE or the JDE Plug-in for Eclipse, you can create several types of BlackBerry projects. We've been making applications up to this point, but there are two others that you may end up using: libraries and alternate entry points.

Libraries

Libraries, like applications, are packaged as .cod files. They're loaded onto a device in the same way. The difference is that they aren't executed directly by the BlackBerry; they contain code or resources used by one or more other applications. You may want to create a library to logically separate your code or to reuse code between applications.

Creating a Library

Creating a library is similar to creating an application. From Eclipse you create a BlackBerry project as normal, and then from the Project Properties, select Library as shown in Figure 3-5.

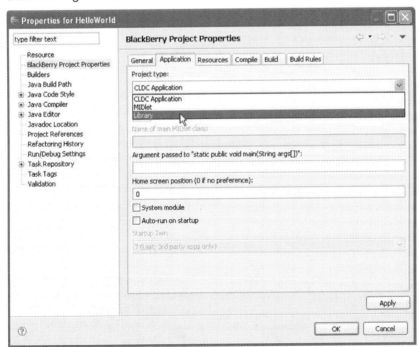

Figure 3-5. *Making a BlackBerry application into a library in Eclipse*

From the JDE, simply select Library from the "Create new file" dialog, as shown in Figure 3-6.

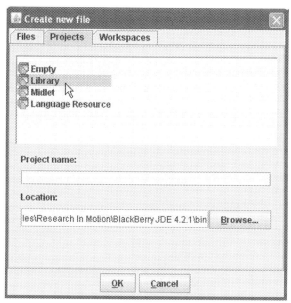

Figure 3-6. *Creating a new Library in the JDE*

Using Libraries in Your Application

Once you have a library, you need to tell your development environment that your application depends on it. From the JDE, this is accomplished through the Project ➤ Dependencies menu item.

From Eclipse, the option is buried a little deeper, under project Properties, select Project References, as shown in Figure 3-7.

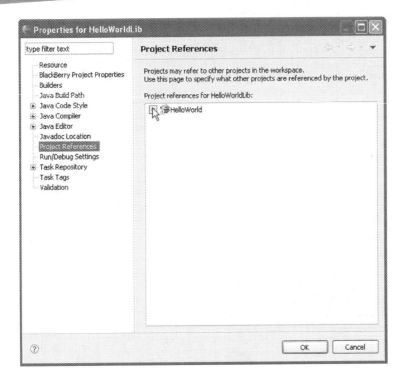

Figure 3-7. *Adding a library dependency from Eclipse*

Once you've added the library dependency to your project, you can refer to classes in that library in the same way as you refer to classes in your application.

NOTE: A warning about duplicate classes on the BlackBerry. The BlackBerry class loader uses one global namespace. This means that having two classes in two different modules have the exact same fully qualified class name will cause a conflict. Having two classes both named `com.beginningblackberry.HelloWorldMainScreen` is a problem, but if one is named `com.somethingelse.HelloWorldMainScreen`, that's OK. Libraries can help you get around naming conflicts like this by moving common code into one place, but they can also cause problems if you're not careful and have the same classes included in a library and in your application.

Creating an Alternate Entry Point

An alternate entry point is exactly what it sounds like—another way for the user or BlackBerry to start your application. An alternate entry point can provide another icon on the BlackBerry home screen to start your application. By clicking on the other icon, the same `main` method is called, but with different parameters, allowing you to run your application in different modes. Alternate entry points are also commonly used with applications that are configured to automatically start when the device powers on or reboots, but that may also need to be started by the user or might be integrated into other applications, such as the Messages or Camera application, and started using a menu item in one of those applications. The process for creating an alternate entry point is fairly similar between the JDE and the JDE Plug-in for Eclipse, so we'll just go over the Eclipse method in this chapter.

In the Hello World workspace, create a new BlackBerry project called HelloWorldAlternate, and open the BlackBerry Project Properties dialog. The Application tab will have a couple of new entries, one of which is Alternate CLDC Application Entry Point. Select that, and the "Alternate entry point for" drop-down will become enabled, letting you select HelloWorld as the project (see Figure 3-8).

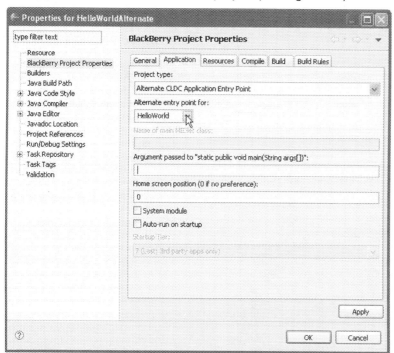

Figure 3-8. *Creating an alternate entry point for the Hello World application*

Let's modify the application a little, so you can see the alternate entry point at work. In the Arguments box, type **alt** and click OK. Now, add a new constructor to HelloWorldMainScreen:

```
public HelloWorldMainScreen(boolean isAlternateEntry) {
    if (isAlternateEntry) {
        labelField = new LabelField("Goodbye World!");
    }
    else {
        labelField = new LabelField("Hello World!");
    }
```

```
        add(labelField);
    }
```

Modify the `main` method and the constructor in `HelloWorldApp` to look at the parameters passed in, and call the alternate constructor if `alt` is the first one:

```
    public static void main(String[] args) {
        HelloWorldApp app = new HelloWorldApp(args);
        app.enterEventDispatcher();
    }

    public HelloWorldApp(String[] args) {
        if (args.length > 0 && args[0].equals("alt")) {
            mainScreen = new HelloWorldMainScreen(true);
        }
        else {
            mainScreen = new HelloWorldMainScreen(false);
        }
        pushScreen(mainScreen);
    }
```

In the new `HelloWorldApp` constructor, we first check the length of `args`. The BlackBerry device will split the argument string that we specified in the project properties for our alternate entry point into words based on whitespace, and place each word into a separate element of the array. Since we didn't specify any arguments for the main `HelloWorld` project, `args` will have a length of 0.

Now when you run the simulator, you'll see a `HelloWorldAlternate` icon on the home screen. Click it, and you'll see Goodbye World, as in Figure 3-9.

Figure 3-9. *Running Hello World through an alternate entry point*

MIDP and MIDlet Projects

Finally, you may have noticed the MIDlet project type in the Eclipse Plug-in or the JDE. In case you're not familiar with Java ME programming, a MIDlet is the application type for the Java ME Mobile Information Device Profile (MIDP), which is essentially a set of classes and capabilities that most Java ME implementations support. Many other types of smartphones from companies such as Nokia, Sony Ericsson, and Motorola support MIDP. You would use MIDP to build applications that run on all these devices without any code changes.

The BlackBerry fully supports MIDP but also includes a large API that's not part of MIDP. This means that the BlackBerry can run MIDlets, and in fact, MIDlets that are specifically built for BlackBerry can access many parts of the non-MIDP API, but they don't have access to the entire BlackBerry API. Specific things that MIDlets do not have access to include the BlackBerry UI API and the BlackBerry application life cycle controls (like automatic start). For these reasons, I recommend that you not write your BlackBerry applications as MIDlets, and in fact, I don't discuss MIDlet-specific topics in this book after this section. However, if you have an existing MIDlet originally built for another smartphone platform and you need to quickly run it on a device, BlackBerry has you covered.

Summary

This chapter has been a bit of a grab bag of interesting development topics, and you'll end up using many of them in your own applications. By now, though, you're probably ready to get back to learning more of the BlackBerry API. So take a deep breath, because now that you have the basic knowledge to create applications, we're going to speed up a bit, and the lessons for the rest of the BlackBerry API are going to start coming fast and furious!

Chapter 4

User Interface Basics

Our Hello World application was great for introducing the BlackBerry development environment and the basics of a BlackBerry application, but it was certainly not what we'd usually think of a as a fully developed application. It lacked the ability to interact with the user, and its user interface was very limited. In the next couple of chapters, we'll explore the BlackBerry user interface in much greater detail and build an application that really shows off what you can do with the BlackBerry.

The BlackBerry API includes a rich framework for building user interfaces for your applications. This chapter will build on the concepts covered in the last two chapters to show you how to use the full range of BlackBerry UI components to build an application with a couple of screens and several controls that respond to user input. We'll also equip the application with a couple of menu items besides the defaults that are provided.

If you're familiar with Java's Abstract Window Toolkit (AWT) Swing, Windows Forms, or another object-oriented user interface toolkit, you'll have no problem learning the BlackBerry UI API. The key point implied here is that user interfaces for Java-based BlackBerry applications are built in code: there are no configuration files or external metadata to worry about. This situation has positive aspects (for example, all UI information is centralized in the Java code) and negative aspects (for example, you have no visual tools for building your UI).

Ready? Let's dive in and start building our application.

The UI Fun Application

We want an application that will show off what the BlackBerry UI can do. We'll build just such an application over the course of this chapter (and improve it in later chapters), but having the end goal in mind before we start will be helpful.

To show off a few of the available controls, and have something with some amount of interactivity, we'll construct a simple login screen. When we're done, the main screen of our application will look like the one shown in Figure 4-1.

Figure 4-1. *Our goal application for this chapter*

There's a plain-text field for the username, a hidden-text password field, a drop-down list that lets the user choose a domain, a check box to ask the application to remember the password, and a couple of buttons that will log in the user and clear the text fields. For good measure, we've thrown in an image at the top of the screen, and we'll add a couple of menu items too.

For this application, there will be no networking; clicking Login will display a simple screen that lets us know that the button has been pressed and shows the credentials the user has entered.

The Components of a BlackBerry UI

All the visible elements on screen in a BlackBerry application are of one of the three types:

- *Fields*: These are the basic building blocks of the UI. Generally, each control, such as a button or text field, corresponds to an instance of a field. The `Field` class draws the control and handles user input.

- *Managers*: These arrange fields on the screen. Each field must belong to one and only one manager. Each manager is also a field, meaning managers can contain other managers, allowing for some pretty intricate UI layouts.

- *Screens*: There's one active screen per application at any time. Screens handle field layout through a delegate manager and provide additional functionality like menus.

Fields are all derived from `net.rim.device.api.ui.Field`. There are a lot of useful prebuilt fields available in the `net.rim.device.api.ui.component` package.

Managers are derived from `net.rim.device.api.ui.Manager`, which you'll find is a subclass of `net.rim.device.api.ui.Field`. Several useful managers are defined in the `net.rim.device.api.ui.container` package.

Screens all derive from `net.rim.device.api.ui.Screen`, which is a subclass of `Manager`, and therefore of `Field`. You'll also find the default screens in the `net.rim.device.api.ui.container` package.

> **NOTE:** Though `Screen` is ultimately descended from `Field`, you can't add a `Screen` to a `Manager`. The hierarchy in this case represents functionality—a `Screen` does things that a `Field` and `Manager` do, such as painting itself, handling user input, and managing fields, but it is not actually a drop-in replacement for a `Field` the way a `Manager` is.

Right now, or at some time soon, you may want to browse through the Javadocs for the packages mentioned in this section. These can give you an idea of what's possible with the BlackBerry and maybe help with some ideas for your own applications. In this chapter, all the fields, managers, and screens we'll use will be those provided with the JDE. You'll learn how to make your own in the next chapter.

Creating the Application

Using your development environment of choice, create a new BlackBerry Application project called UiFun. We'll create the application class and main screen class as before. The main application class will be the same as the simple first version that we created a couple of chapters ago. We'll use the package `com.beginningblackberry.uifun` and call the application and main screen classes `UiFunApplication` and `UiFunMainScreen`. You should know enough to create these classes now, but for reference the source code follows:

```
package com.beginningblackberry.uifun;
import net.rim.device.api.ui.UiApplication;

public class UiFunApplication extends UiApplication {
    public UiFunApplication() {
        UiFunMainScreen mainScreen = new UiFunMainScreen();
        pushScreen(mainScreen);
    }

    public static void main(String[] args) {
        UiFunApplication app = new UiFunApplication();
        app.enterEventDispatcher();
    }
```

```
}
```

Here's the source code for the UiFun application class:

```
package com.beginningblackberry.uifun;

import net.rim.device.api.ui.container.MainScreen;

public class UiFunMainScreen extends MainScreen {
    public UiFunMainScreen() {

    }
}
```

Adding the Logo Image

The first field we add will be an instance of
`net.rim.device.api.ui.component.BitmapField` to show the image at the top of
the screen.

The BlackBerry can use PNG, GIF, or JPEG images, but most applications use PNGs
because of their reduced size, high quality, and support for transparencies. When
creating images for use in your application, always consider compressing your image as
much as possible using your graphics program or a PNG optimizer (several good free
ones are available), because large images can very quickly increase the size of your
application. You can download the logo image we're using from the book's web site at
`http://www.beginningblackberry.com`.

Adding the Image to the Project

If you're using the JDE Plug-in for Eclipse, add the image file to your Eclipse project by
creating a new folder called `res` at the same level as your source folder (see Figure 4-2),
copying the image into that folder and from your Eclipse workspace by right-clicking
your project and clicking Refresh. You can put images in whatever folder you want,
ut for this example, we decided to create a specific resources folder (hence the
name `res`).

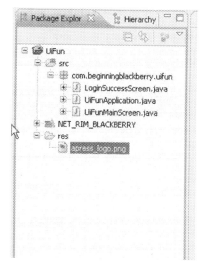

Figure 4-2. *This Eclipse workspace with the apress_logo.png image added*

If you're using the stand-alone JDE, create a folder called `res` at the same level as your `com` folder (the root of your source tree), and copy the image file there (see Figure 4-3). Then, from the Project menu, choose Add File to Project, and browse to the image file.

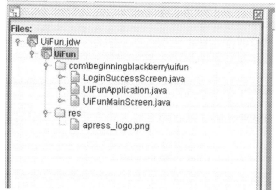

Figure 4-3. *The JDE workspace with the apress_logo.png image added*

Adding the Image to the Screen

`BitmapField` takes a `Bitmap` object as an argument in its constructor, so we'll need to load the image before constructing the field. We'll import `net.rim.device.api.system.Bitmap` and add the following line to `UiFunMainScreen`'s constructor load the bitmap from the image resource we just added:

```
Bitmap logoBitmap = Bitmap.getBitmapResource("res/apress_log.png");
```

The path for loading bitmaps, and all other resources, is relative to the location of your project definition file (the .jdp file). We put the bitmap in a res folder at the same level as our src folder.

Finally, we want to center the bitmap horizontally at the top of the screen. MainScreen lays out fields vertically top to bottom in the order that they're added, so the BitmapField will automatically appear at the top of the screen. But to horizontally center it, we need to specify the Field.FIELD_HCENTER style in its constructor. We've also elected to make the BitmapField a member field instead of just declaring it locally in the constructor. We'll follow this pattern for all our fields—making our user interface components member fields will become important as we start to handle user input.

Now, constructing the bitmap field and adding it to the screen is easy. The complete code follows:

```
package com.beginningblackberry.uifun;

import net.rim.device.api.system.Bitmap;
import net.rim.device.api.ui.Field;
import net.rim.device.api.ui.component.BitmapField;
import net.rim.device.api.ui.container.MainScreen;

public class UiFunMainScreen extends MainScreen {
    BitmapField bitmapField;

    public UiFunMainScreen() {
        Bitmap logoBitmap = Bitmap.getBitmapResource("res/apress_logo.png");
        bitmapField = new BitmapField(logoBitmap, Field.FIELD_HCENTER);
        add(bitmapField);
    }
}
```

And when this code is run, we'll see the screen shown in Figure 4-4.

Figure 4-4. *The BitmapField centered at the top of the screen*

Field Style Flags

Almost all fields and managers have a constructor that takes a style parameter. The style is a mask of various style flags concatenated with the bitwise or operator (|). These flags are defined throughout the API, although most are in Field and Manager, and they can influence many different aspects of field appearance, positioning, and behavior. You can apply any style to any field, but whether the style has an effect depends on the field and sometimes the manager that contains that field. Generally, anything defined within the Field class is applicable to any field (including managers); anything defined within the Manager class is applicable to any manager, and anything defined within the Screen class is applicable to any screen. Flags defined within a specific subclass of field usually only apply to that field and any field that subclasses it; examples include the ButtonField.CONSUME_CLICK style and the various styles associated with TextField, BasicEditField, and their subclasses.

There are unfortunately no guarantees about how a specific style flag will affect different fields. Generally, flags work the way you'd expect them to, but remember that just setting a particular alignment flag on a field does not guarantee that you'll get exactly what you want. For example, some managers ignore the alignment flags, which will become clear when we build our own manager later on.

The Javadocs provide more information for specific fields.

Adding a Few More Fields

Next, we'll add our screen's remaining controls: the username and password fields, the domain drop-down list, the check box, and the Login and Clear buttons.

Creating the Username and Password Fields

We'll use an `EditField` for the username and a `PasswordEditField` (which automatically hides characters as they are typed) for the password field. Each of these fields can display its own label, specified in the constructor. We don't need to apply any special styles to these fields.

Add the following import statement to the top of `UiFunMainScreen.java`, just under the other import statements:

```
import net.rim.device.api.ui.component.EditField;
```

Then, add the following declarations to the top of the `UiFunMainScreen` class:

```
EditField usernameField;
PasswordEditField passwordField;
```

And add the following lines go in the constructor:

```
usernameField = new EditField("Username:", "");
passwordField = new PasswordEditField("Password:", "");
add(usernameField);
add(passwordField);
```

Creating the Domain Field and Check Box

The Domain field should be a drop-down list. For the BlackBerry, this is accomplished by an instance of `net.rim.device.api.ui.component.ChoiceField`. You can implement the interface directly, but for this application, the `net.rim.device.api.ui.component. ObjectChoiceField` component will do just fine; it allows us to specify an array of `Objects`, which will be used to populate the field (the `toString` method will be used for the display string). If you want a list of numbers, `net.rim.device.api.ui.component. NumericChoiceField` is also often useful.

We'll add the imports for both of these fields first:

```
import net.rim.device.api.ui.component.CheckboxField;
import net.rim.device.api.ui.component.ObjectChoiceField;
```

Then, we add the declaration of the member variables, again at the top of the `UiFunMainScreen` class:

```
ObjectChoiceField domainField;
CheckboxField rememberCheckbox;
```

Because we're just using hard-coded values for this application, instantiating our `ObjectChoiceField` is easy:

```
domainField = new ObjectChoiceField("Domain:", new String[] {"Home", "Work"});
add(domainField);
```

And by this point, you can probably figure out how to use `net.rim.device.api.ui.component.CheckboxField` to create a check box on screen; there's nothing special to note about `CheckboxField` except that you have to specify the state of the check box (`true` for checked or `false` for unchecked) when you instantiate it:

```
rememberCheckbox = new CheckboxField("Remember password", false);
add(rememberCheckbox);
```

Creating the Buttons

To create the Login and Clear buttons that go beneath these text fields, we'll use—as you might expect—the `ButtonField` class. A warning with `ButtonFields`: when creating a `ButtonField`, you should always specify the style `ButtonField.CONSUME_CLICK`. If you don't, the click event will be passed onto the screen, and a menu will open when the user clicks the button, though your button will still cause an action to be performed.

First, we'll import `ButtonField`:

```
import net.rim.device.api.ui.component.ButtonField;;
```

Next, we add the declarations for our two buttons:

```
    ButtonField clearButton;
    ButtonField loginButton;
```

Finally, the following lines go in the `UiFunMainScreen` constructor:

```
clearButton = new ButtonField("Clear", ButtonField.CONSUME_CLICK);
loginButton = new ButtonField("Login", ButtonField.CONSUME_CLICK);
add(clearButton);
add(loginButton);
```

Now, if you run the application, you'll see something similar to Figure 4-5.

Figure 4-5. *The fields for the UiFun application*

We're pretty close to being done! But we want those two buttons to be beside each other instead of one on top of the other.

Arranging the Buttons Horizontally

Remember that MainScreen (which UiFunMainScreen is derived from) lays out its fields vertically. To put two fields beside each other, we need to place them in an instance of net.rim.device.api.ui.container.HorizontalFieldManager and add that manager to the screen. We'll give the HorizontalFieldManager the Field.FIELD_RIGHT style, to put the buttons on the right side of the screen.

Add the following import:

```
import net.rim.device.api.ui.container.HorizontalFieldManager;
```

Erase the two add calls for the buttons, and replace them with this:

```
HorizontalFieldManager buttonManager = new HorizontalFieldManager(Field.FIELD_RIGHT);
buttonManager.add(clearButton);
buttonManager.add(loginButton);
add(buttonManager);
```

We'll also add a couple of instances of net.rim.device.api.ui.component.SeparatorField, which draws a horizontal line across the screen, and of LabelField, which contains our login instructions. The full code for the UiFunMainScreen constructor at this point follows (remember to add an import statement for SeparatorField):

```
Bitmap logoBitmap = Bitmap.getBitmapResource("res/apress_logo.png");
bitmapField = new BitmapField(logoBitmap, Field.FIELD_HCENTER);
add(bitmapField);
add(new SeparatorField());
add(new LabelField("Please enter your credentials:"));

usernameField = new EditField("Username:", "");
passwordField = new PasswordEditField("Password:", "");
add(usernameField);
add(passwordField);

domainField = new ObjectChoiceField("Domain:", new String[] {"Home", "Work"});
add(domainField);

rememberCheckbox = new CheckboxField("Remember password:", false);
add(rememberCheckbox);

add(new SeparatorField());

clearButton = new ButtonField("Clear", ButtonField.CONSUME_CLICK);
loginButton = new ButtonField("Login", ButtonField.CONSUME_CLICK);

HorizontalFieldManager buttonManager =
  new HorizontalFieldManager(Field.FIELD_RIGHT);
buttonManager.add(clearButton);
buttonManager.add(loginButton);
add(buttonManager);
}
```

Running the application, we'll see our screen looking the way we intended it, as
Figure 4-6 illustrates.

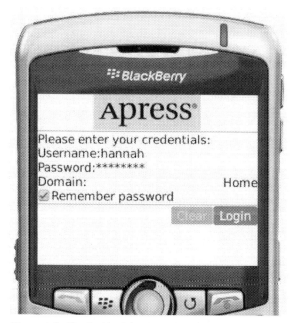

Figure 4-6. *The final look for the login screen*

Handling User Interaction

Now, we have a screen that looks the way we want it to, but it doesn't do anything yet—well, you can move the focus between controls, type in the text fields, and change the check box and the choice field, but the application doesn't *really* do anything yet. Let's get those buttons to work!

Handling UI Events

The BlackBerry API uses an observer pattern to dispatch events: All fields can have a listener attached to them, and that listener is notified when a change event happens. The exact trigger for a change event varies from field to field.

In the case of ButtonField, the change event happens when the button is clicked by the trackball or a touch on the touch screen, or when the Enter key is pressed while a button is highlighted. For CheckboxField, a change event happens when the check box is checked or unchecked, and for ChoiceField, an event happens whenever the user selects a different choice.

You attach a listener using the Field.setChangeListener method.

Note that the BlackBerry provides a unicast event model: there is only ever at most one change listener for a field. If you use Field.setChangeListener, you replace whatever listener may have been there already, preventing it from receiving events. This makes a lot of sense for a mobile platform where resources and application scope are limited but may be different from what you're used to with desktop or server application development.

A listener must implement the FieldChangeListener interface. In this case, we'll make our UiFunMainScreen implement net.rim.device.api.ui.FieldChangeListener by changing the class declaration and implementing the listener method in UiFunMainScreen:

```
public class UiFunMainScreen extends MainScreen implements FieldChangeListener {
public void fieldChanged(Field field, int context) {
}
```

Remember to add an import for net.rim.device.api.ui.FieldChangeListener to the top of the Java file.

The field parameter is a reference to the field that originated the change, in this case, one of our ButtonField instances (once we've added them). The context can mean different things: when you define your own fields, you can use it to pass along additional information about the field change event. For this application, we'll ignore the context parameter.

Handling the Clear Button

We'll hook up the Clear button first. Add the following line in the constructor, just after instantiating the button:

```
clearButton.setChangeListener(this);
```

Now, when the user clicks on the clear button, we'll receive an event in `UiFunMainScreen.fieldChanged`. We can test this with a simple dialog using the `net.rim.device.api.ui.component.Dialog` class:

```
public void fieldChanged(Field field, int context) {
    if (field == clearButton) {
        Dialog.inform("Clear Button Pressed!");
    }
}
```

The `Dialog` class is a handy way of displaying simple messages to the user. Run the application, and click Clear to see that we're correctly handling and receiving the event (see Figure 4-7).

Figure 4-7. *An event from the Clear button*

Of course, what we actually want the Clear button to do is remove all text from our fields. Let's define a method to do this. Add the following to `UiFunMainScreen`:

```
private void clearTextFields() {
    usernameField.setText("");
    passwordField.setText("");
}
```

And change the `fieldChanged` method to call our new method:

```
public void fieldChanged(Field field, int context) {
    if (field == clearButton) {
        clearTextFields();
    }
}
```

Now, clicking Clear will erase the text from both of our fields (see Figure 4-8).

Figure 4-8. *When the fields are populated (as in the image on the left), clicking the Clear button removes the text from the fields (as shown in the image on the right).*

Handling the Login Button

We'll do two things with our Login button: Check that both fields have some text in them and display a warning dialog if they don't. And, if both have been filled in, display a new screen informing the user that login was successful.

Defining a New Screen

To keep the flow of everything fairly logical, let's define the login success screen now. It will be a simple screen with three label fields, one each to show a successful login, the username, and the selected domain. We'll pass the username and domain in the constructor of the screen. The entire code for `LoginSuccessScreen` is as follows:

```
package com.beginningblackberry.uifun;

import net.rim.device.api.ui.component.LabelField;
import net.rim.device.api.ui.container.MainScreen;
```

```
public class LoginSuccessScreen extends MainScreen {
    public LoginSuccessScreen(String username, String domain) {
        add(new LabelField("Logged in!"));
        add(new LabelField("Username: " + username));
        add(new LabelField("Domain: " + domain));
    }
}
```

We display the new screen in the same way as we displayed UiFunMainScreen from UiFunApplication, but here, we have to get a reference to our UiApplication instance first. UiApplication.getUiApplication() will give us that; in fact, it's a reference to the very same instance of UiFunApplication that we created in our main method. The code will look something like this:

```
LoginSuccessScreen loginSuccessScreen = new LoginSuccessScreen(…)
UiApplication.getUiApplication().pushScreen(loginSuccessScreen);
```

As we did with the Clear button, we'll define a method to perform the login logic described previously. We need the name of the selected domain to pass to the new screen; we can get the index of the currently selected item in domainField by calling domainField.getSelectedIndex(), and we can get the choice associated with that index by calling domainField.getChoice(int). The getChoice method returns an Object. However, because all the objects we passed into the constructor for domainField were Strings, we can safely cast the result of getChoice back to a String. The full code for UiFunMainScreen.login follows:

```
private void login() {
    if (usernameField.getTextLength() == 0 || passwordField.getTextLength() == 0) {
        Dialog.alert("You must enter a username and password");
    }
    else {
        String username = usernameField.getText();
        String selectedDomain =
            (String)domainField.getChoice(domainField.getSelectedIndex());
        LoginSuccessScreen loginSuccessScreen =
            new LoginSuccessScreen(username, selectedDomain);
        UiApplication.getUiApplication().pushScreen(loginSuccessScreen);
    }
}
```

We'll have to modify fieldChanged to handle the login button as well:

```
public void fieldChanged(Field field, int context) {
    if (field == clearButton) {
        clearTextFields();
    }
    else if (field == loginButton) {
        login();
    }
}
```

Finally, remember to add the change listener to loginButton in UiFunMainScreen's constructor:

```
loginButton.setChangeListener(this);
```

When you run the application now, you'll see the result show in Figure 4-9.

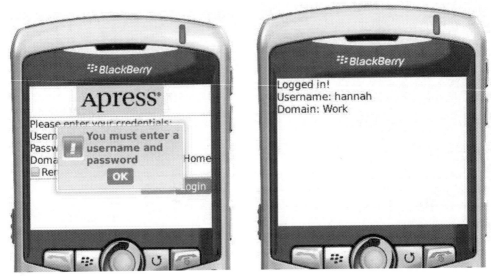

Figure 4-9. *Clicking Login without a username a password (left) and with a username and password (right)*

Creating Menus

Menus are everywhere in a BlackBerry application; in fact, you should try to provide menu options for most major functionality, because the menu is easier to access on most BlackBerry devices than buttons on the screen.

The screen handles displaying menus, and menu items contain their own logic for performing actions.

Understanding Menu Items

Individual items in a menu are instances of net.rim.device.api.ui.MenuItem. This class is abstract, and implements Runnable (it has a run method that you need to implement). The run method is executed on the event thread when the user clicks the menu item, so you can safely modify the UI from within the run method. This also means you shouldn't do any heavy processing or networking in the run method without starting a separate thread.

Each menu item has three pieces of information associated with it: text to display, a *priority*, and an *ordinal*. The priority determines which menu item is initially highlighted when the menu is first displayed; the item with the lowest value for priority will be highlighted when the menu is first opened. The ordinal determines where the item will appear in the menu relative to other menu items. A menu item will appear above menu items with higher ordinal values and below menu items with lower ordinal values. Two menu items with the same ordinal will appear in the order they were added to the menu, top to bottom.

Implementing the Login and Clear Menu Items

We'll implement two menu items for our application corresponding to the Login and Clear actions.

We'll create a new class for each menu item and declare these as inner classes within UiFunMainScreen—because we'll only use them here and to give them access to UiFunMainScreen's private login and clearTextFields methods:

```java
public class UiFunMainScreen extends MainScreen implements FieldChangeListener {
    class LoginMenuItem extends MenuItem {
        public LoginMenuItem() {
            super("Login", 20, 10);
        }

        public void run() {
            login();
        }
    }

    class ClearMenuItem extends MenuItem {
        public ClearMenuItem() {
            super("Clear", 10, 20);
        }

        public void run() {
            clearTextFields();
        }
    }
}
```

Notice how we arranged the ordinal and priorities with the menu items. ClearMenuItem has a lower ordinal value and higher priority value than LoginMenuItem. Therefore, Clear will appear above Login on the menu, but Login will be highlighted by default. This arrangement lets us mirror the order of the buttons on screen, but make the most likely user choice the default one, saving our users a bit of time.

There are a couple of places we can add menu items. One is in the screen's constructor, by calling getMenu and adding items to the Menu object we get back. The other is by overriding makeMenu in our screen class. We'll do the latter, because makeMenu is useful when creating context sensitive menus (menus whose items may change depending on the state of the screen). The makeMenu method in UiFunMainScreen should look like this:

```java
protected void makeMenu(Menu menu, int instance) {
    super.makeMenu(menu, instance);
    menu.add(new LoginMenuItem());
    menu.add(new ClearMenuItem());
}
```

It's very important to have the super.makeMenu call here; otherwise, the default menu items for the screen will not be added. Specifically, we'd lose the Close item that MainScreen automatically adds for us. There are times where we might want to change that, but not for this application, so we'll be sure to make the super.makeMenu call.

One final tip—we declared the menu items explicitly as classes in this example to present things in a clear order, but you'll usually see menu items declared as anonymous inner classes instead. Using an anonymous inner class is more succinct, and you generally use each menu item class only once in a given application. So instead of using the preceding implementation, we could have omitted the declarations for LoginMenuItem and ClearMenuItem and instead done the following in makeMenu:

```
protected void makeMenu(Menu menu, int instance) {
    super.makeMenu(menu, instance);
    menu.add(new MenuItem("Login", 20, 10) {
        public void run() {
            login();
        }
    });
    menu.add(new MenuItem("Clear", 10, 20) {
        public void run() {
            clearTextFields();
        }
    });
}
```

In fact, we'll be using this form throughout the rest of this book.

Supporting Different Menu Instances

The instance parameter is used to identify which menu we're supposed to show. BlackBerry applications display a few slightly different menus depending on how the menu is displayed and the context of the screen and controls. The defined instances follow:

- Menu.INSTANCE_CONTEXT: The menu was displayed by clicking the trackball. Usually, this menu will be a subset of only the items available in the default menu that are applicable to the currently focused control or section of the screen. For example, Close wouldn't show up here. The BlackBerry automatically adds a Full Menu item to this menu, which causes makeMenu to be called with INSTANCE_DEFAULT as the instance parameter.

- Menu.INSTANCE_CONTEXT_SELECTION: This is the same as INSTANCE_CONTEXT, but the menu is displayed while the user has some text selected. You can use this to display items that may only apply when you can copy text.

- Menu.INSTANCE_DEFAULT: In this case, menu is displayed by pressing the menu key. This menu should contain all the items in the context menu, in addition to any items that apply to the application as a whole. Close would show up here.

In our application, we want Login and Clear to show up no matter which control has focus, since everything is related to logging in. Effectively, we can ignore the instance parameter in makeMenu, as the BlackBerry will automatically take care of putting the

Close item only in the appropriate menu instance. This is why our makeMenu method is so simple.

With that discussion out of the way, we can now run the application and see our menu items, which should look like the ones in Figures 4-10 and 4-11.

Figure 4-10. *In the context menu, notice the Login is selected, and the Full Menu item is present.*

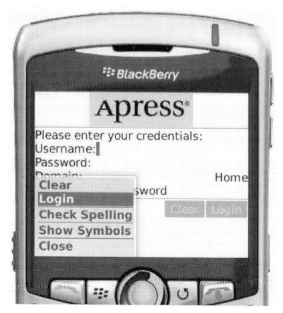

Figure 4-11. *In the default menu, notice the Login is selected, and many more menu items are present.*

You'll notice that the instance menu can only show up when the currently focused control does not consume the click. Our ButtonFields have the ButtonField.CONSUME_CLICK style flag set, so the instance menu won't show up when you click the trackball while they're focused, which is how you'd expect buttons to behave. The CheckboxField and ObjectChoiceField also consume the trackball click, so we'll see the context menu only when we click the trackball on one of the text fields.

Clicking either the Clear or Login menu item will have the same effect as clicking the Clear or Login button.

Summary

Congratulations, you've created your first multiscreen, interactive BlackBerry application! Although the application was simple, we covered a lot of ground in this chapter. You should now understand how to construct a BlackBerry UI using screens, managers, and fields and how to support user interaction through controls and menus.

The concepts that we covered are basically the same as those you'll use to construct UIs of any complexity in Java-based BlackBerry applications, and they are fundamentally important to any BlackBerry developer. So, if there was anything you didn't understand fully, go back and review that section. Moving on from this chapter with a gap in your understanding will slow you down as we get into creating more advanced applications in later chapters.

Using just what you've learned so far, you can construct some fairly complex applications, although they'd be a bit limited in usefulness without networking or persistent storage. We'll tackle both of those topics in later chapters, but before that, the next chapter will go even deeper into the API and create some custom fields, managers, and screens to really remove any limits and let you create almost any user interface you can design and imagine.

Chapter 5

Beyond the Basics of User Interfaces

The previous chapter introduced the major concepts that you'll need to build a BlackBerry user interface. Armed with what you learned, you can create a wide range of very functional applications. In this chapter, we'll take a deeper dive into the BlackBerry API and learn how to really control all aspects of the look and feel of your application's UI.

The topics in this chapter will get a bit more advanced but are nothing you shouldn't be able to handle if you've followed through up to this point. I'll be up front though, and say that you've already learned enough to put together a user interface that could support a lot of different applications, so if you want to skip over this chapter for now and go on to learn about networking, persistence, and other services before spending time on your UI, then go ahead. Later topics don't depend on this chapter, so skipping it for now won't do any harm. I highly recommend that you do come back here before finally publishing your application, as the topics we'll cover here will go a long way toward improving the appearance and overall user experience of your application.

In this chapter, we'll take the UI Fun application that we built in the last chapter as a starting point and modify a lot of the components that make up its user interface. We'll focus a bit on some aspects of the API that we glossed over earlier (yes, I know we did) and explore fonts, colors, and more; this will give you a feel for what can be done, but of course, as with all things in this book, you should just look at this as the beginning. When you're done here, you'll have the tools and knowledge to implement almost any user interface that you can imagine and design.

Enhancing the UI Fun Application

We're starting with the UI Fun application from Chapter 4. If you didn't go through that entire chapter and build the application, we recommend you do that before continuing, to make sure you've got the solid hold on the UI fundamentals that you'll need in this chapter. If you believe you're comfortable enough but didn't go all the way through, you can download the complete source code to the Chapter 4 version of UiFun from this book's web site.

Chapter 10

Next Steps

We've come quite a way since starting out on our journey. You may have started with little or no knowledge of how to develop BlackBerry applications, but by this point you should be familiar with the basics of developing user interfaces and creating applications that use—among other things—persistent storage, wireless networking, and location-based services.

At this point, you're more than ready to start building the application of your dreams, but of course there's always more to know. The BlackBerry platform has been around for a while and has changed quite a bit in that time. It continues to evolve today—like the rest of the mobile world—at a faster pace than ever. BlackBerry App World is the first of many great additions to the platform that will come to the platform in the next while.

Mobile application development is still in its infancy, and BlackBerry is going to be around and growing with the mobile industry for a long time. So, part of your job as a BlackBerry developer will be staying on top of everything that happens, learning and evaluating new platform capabilities, and seeing if the new features would make your applications even better.

Keeping Up-to-Date

The main source for up-to-date information about BlackBerry is the first one I mentioned in this book, the BlackBerry Developer Zone:

`http://www.blackberry.com/developers`

Along with being the source for all your BlackBerry application development tools, the Resources section contains a lot of useful information and should be among the first places you turn to get a question answered:

`http://www.blackberry.com/developers/resources`

Among other things, the knowledge base, developer documentation (including development guidelines, white papers, and online versions of the Javadocs), tutorials, and videos are all very useful.

Working with Fonts

The first and easiest thing to do will be to change the font used in the UI components. The BlackBerry platform includes pretty good font support and makes it almost trivial to change the font used for a component or an entire screen.

Font support is provided through the net.rim.device.api.ui.Font and FontFamily classes. Through these, you can create fonts using any of the fonts installed on your device (quite a collection for all recent BlackBerry devices).

There are two ways to get a font. One is to obtain a specific font family (what might be called a typeface in different systems) and get a specific font from it. The other is to derive a font from another font you already have.

To get font from a font family, we must have an instance of that font family; this just involves the FontFamily.forName method. You can use any of the names of the families on your device – you can see these on the device by going to the device's options screen, and selecting Screen/Keyboard (see Figure 5-3). This also gives you a nice real-time preview of different font families, styles, and sizes.

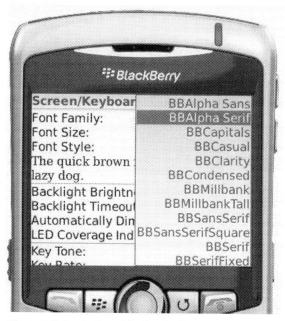

Figure 5-3. A selection of the font families available on a BlackBerry device

To demonstrate BlackBerry font support, we'll explicitly set a new font for UiFun. Starting with the code as at the end of Chapter 4, add the following imports to the top of UiFunMainScreen.java:

```
import net.rim.device.api.ui.Font;
import net.rim.device.api.ui.FontFamily;
import net.rim.device.api.ui.Ui;
```

The Ui class will be used in a minute; we've just added the import statement here to save time. We'll use the BB Alpha Serif family, available on all devices, to more closely match the lettering in our logo image. Add the following to the UiFunMainScreen constructor:

```
try {
        FontFamily alphaSerifFamily = FontFamily.forName("BBAlpha Serif");
    } catch (ClassNotFoundException e) {
    }
```

This method won't ever actually throw a ClassNotFoundException, though it's a checked exception so the Java language requires us to add some code to handle it. If you specify a name for a font family that isn't available, the BlackBerry will still return a default.

There are a few choices for font style (the standard bold, italic, underlined, and so on), defined as constants in the Font class. You can also specify font sizes in a few different ways; the main ones to be concerned with are points and pixels. The size unit is specified using one of the constants from the net.rim.device.api.ui.Ui class.

For our application, we'll use a 9-point plain (not bold, italic, or underlined) version of BB Alpha Serif:

```
Font appFont = alphaSerifFamily.getFont(Font.PLAIN, 9, Ui.UNITS_pt);
```

NOTE: Font sizes should generally be specified as points instead of pixels, because BlackBerry devices vary a great deal in screen resolution and physical size, or in other words, in dots per inch (DPI). A 10-pixel font may be acceptable on a BlackBerry Pearl but will look tiny on the higher resolution screen of a Curve 8900. Using points makes the fonts appear roughly the same physical size on these different devices.

Changing the screen's font is straightforward:

```
setFont(appFont);
```

All the font code, added to UiFunMainScreen's constructor, looks like this:

```
public UiFunMainScreen() {
    try {
        FontFamily alphaSansFamily = FontFamily.forName("BBAlpha Serif");
        Font appFont = alphaSansFamily.getFont(Font.PLAIN, 9, Ui.UNITS_pt);
        setFont(appFont);
    } catch (ClassNotFoundException e) {
    }
    // ...
}
```

Each screen, manager, and field can have a different font, but setting the font for a container (screen or manager) will generally have the effect of setting the font for everything contained within it, unless you specify a different font for some of the components using *their* setFont methods. All this means that we don't have to do anything else, and we've now specified a different font for all the controls in our application. Run UiFun, and you'll see the new font in effect (see Figure 5-4).

Figure 5-4. *All elements, including text typed into the edit fields, are now using the new the BB Alpha Serif font.*

Drawing to the Screen Using the Graphics Context

The basic interface for displaying anything to the BlackBerry device's screen is the net.rim.device.api.ui.Graphics class. It's used under the hood by pretty much all elements of the BlackBerry user interface, and it gives you the tools to do anything you've seen in any BlackBerry application's user interface. If you're going to be doing any kind of user interface work with BlackBerry applications, you should get very familiar with the Graphics class.

Each instance of Graphics is associated either with a Bitmap object or with a display (basically, a BlackBerry device's physical screen). For this book, we'll only focus on a Graphics object associated with a display.

Using the paint method

All fields (and managers and screens) get access to the Graphics object associated with the current display through the paint method. This method is called whenever the BlackBerry device determines that the section of the display containing the Field needs repainting. An important thing to bear in mind is that *the same instance of the* Graphics class is used by *all* managers and fields on a screen, and this instance is passed by the screen through its managers to the fields. This may seem a minor point, but it's important to keep in mind, as it'll help in determining exactly why your application is drawing to the screen in a certain way. For example, setting the color on the Graphics object will affect the color of components drawn after it, unless they explicitly set their own colors.

Because it's so important to understand how the UI is displayed by the BlackBerry platform, we'll take time for a brief discussion here before getting to more concrete examples.

Understanding How the BlackBerry Screen Is Drawn

At a high level, things happen in two stages. First comes the *layout* stage, where `layout` and `sublayout` methods are called and all the fields are positioned and sized on the screen. Second is the *paint* stage, where `paint` methods are called and the fields actually draw to the display.

Laying Out the Screen

Layout involves positioning and sizing all the managers and controls on the screen. It starts with the screen itself and works down through all the nested managers and fields as follows:

1. The screen's `sublayout(int width, int height)` method is called. The `width` and `height` parameters will be the width and height in pixels of the device's display.

2. The `sublayout` method of the screen's *delegate manager* is called. You'll learn more about the delegate manager when you learn to build your own screen class, but briefly, it's the component that actually contains and lays out all the fields and managers on the screen and is the only component directly controlled by the `Screen` itself. Often, the delegate manager will take up the entire screen, but there are instances, such as in a dialog with a border, where this may not be the case. So the `width` and `height` parameters passed to the delegate manager's `sublayout` method will be less than or equal to the `width` and `height` parameters passed to the screen's `sublayout` method.

3. The delegate manager iterates through all the fields and managers it contains and lays out each of them, that is, positions them within itself, tells them how much space is potentially available and asks them what size they'll be on screen. This has the effect of calling `sublayout` (for a manager) or `layout` (for a field). The width and height available to each of the fields and managers will vary depending on how the delegate manager lays out its fields. In many cases, they may be greater than the height and width of the delegate manager itself; this means that the delegate manager is a scrolling manager and will only draw a subset of its fields at any time.

4. Each manager lays out its managers, fields, and so on.

5. Each field lays out itself out; a field may take up less than the space available.

Painting to the Screen

The Painting stage is where pixels are actually drawn to the screen. In the same sequence as the layout stage, the screen, managers and fields are all asked to paint themselves:

1. The screen's `paint` method is called, with a Graphics context that represents the current display.

2. The screen may do some painting itself (drawing its background for example) and then asks its delegate manager to paint itself, which has the effect of calling the delegate manager's paint method with the same Graphics object. If the delegate manager is smaller than the screen, the screen will set a clipping region on the Graphics object to the size and position of the delegate. This prevents the delegate from drawing outside its size (set during layout) and frees the delegate from worrying about what its absolute position on screen is (which, in fact, it generally doesn't know).

3. The delegate manager again may do some painting itself, and then asks each of its subfields and managers to paint themselves, setting appropriate clipping regions for each of its fields.

4. Each manager paints itself and asks its managers and fields to paint themselves.

5. Each field paints itself.

Another important thing to keep in mind is that layout happens rarely—generally when a screen is constructed or when fields are added or removed—while paint happens frequently. This means that you should be very concerned about the speed of your paint methods; slow paint methods will slow down your user interface and negatively affect your application's user experience.

You should remember, in a nutshell, that

*   Layout happens once (or rarely), and in this step fields size themselves and are positioned.

*   Paint happens often, and in this step, fields draw their contents to the display.

Now that we've covered the framework, it's time to fill in the details by actually implementing some custom fields, managers, and screens. Along the way, we'll use a lot of the methods in the Graphics class and explore those as we encounter them.

Creating Custom Fields

We'll create a couple of custom fields, first a simple static noninteractive one to introduce the concepts and then a more complicated one that deals with user interaction, focus, and events.

Adding a Custom Label Field

We'll start by replacing the Please Enter Your Credentials field with one built from scratch that will use different foreground and background colors and contain a small image. It's a simple field to make but will illustrate the basic concepts well.

Creating the Basic Field Class

Create a new class under the com.beginningblackberry.uifun package called CustomLabelField that subclasses net.rim.device.api.ui.Field. Here's the basic outline, with placeholders for the two abstract methods that we're required to implement for any field:

```
package com.beginningblackberry.uifun;

import net.rim.device.api.ui.Field;
import net.rim.device.api.ui.Graphics;
import net.rim.device.api.system.Bitmap;
import net.rim.device.api.ui.DrawStyle;

public class CustomLabelField extends Field {

    protected void layout(int width, int height) {
    }

    protected void paint(Graphics graphics) {
    }
}
```

Bitmap and DrawStyle will be used by the field a bit later; we just added the import statements now for convenience.

Creating a Constructor

We'll now add a constructor and a few member variables to contain the label text and foreground and background colors (we'll add the image shortly):

```
    private String label;
    private int foregroundColor;
    private int backgroundColor;

    public CustomLabelField(String label, int foregroundColor,
            int backgroundColor, long style) {
        super(style);
        this.label = label;
```

```
    this.foregroundColor = foregroundColor;
    this.backgroundColor = backgroundColor;
    }
```

> **NOTE:** Colors on the BlackBerry are represented by `ints`. You can use one of the constants in the `net.rim.device.api.ui.Color` class to select a desired color, or specify a color in hexadecimal RRGGBB format, the same as in HTML, such as 0xFF0000 for red or 0x0000FF for blue.

The BlackBerry actually uses a 16-bit color model, with 5 bits for red, 6 for green, and 5 for blue. It'll automatically select the closest color to whichever one you specify, but it may not appear exactly as on screen, and the apparent color can vary from device to device depending on screen characteristics. So be sure to test out your color choices on a range of real devices.

One final thing to notice in the constructor; we've added a style parameter so the user of this field can set styles. It's a good idea when creating fields to provide at least one constructor where style flags can be set.

Adding the layout Method

We'll do something very simple for the `layout` method. Since we want our label field to span the width of the screen, we'll just use the passed-in `width` parameter as our field width. Remember the `width` parameter tells how much space is available to our field. We'll base the height on the height of the `Field`'s font:

```
    protected void layout(int width, int height) {
        setExtent(width, getFont().getHeight());
    }
```

Although it's a simple method, there's an important principle illustrated here: Because there are a wide range of BlackBerry models, and default fonts and screen resolutions vary quite a bit, you should avoid specifying absolute sizes wherever possible. Instead, you should specify everything relative to the widths and heights available to you at runtime, including the widths and heights of the fonts being used. This will help a great deal in getting your application to run on a different model of BlackBerry. By doing things this way, we could go back and select a different font for our screen, and we wouldn't have to change this layout method.

After calling `setExtent`, the `getWidth` and `getHeight` methods in our field will return the values we set; this is how the manager containing this field will now how to lay out our field in relation to all the other fields it manages and how it will know how much space to give the field to paint.

Adding the paint Method

To draw text to the display, we can just use the following:

```
protected void paint(Graphics graphics) {
    graphics.drawText(label, 0, 0);
}
```

We don't have to worry about setting a specific font. The Graphics object will have its font set to the field's current font, meaning that the font that we set earlier in UiFunMainScreen is already the current font for this graphics object.

Now, let's set the foreground and background colors and make sure we clear the field to the background color before we draw the text:

```
protected void paint(Graphics graphics) {
    graphics.setBackgroundColor(backgroundColor);
    graphics.clear();
    graphics.setColor(foregroundColor);
    graphics.drawText(label, 0, 0);
}
```

And that's almost everything we need to do; in fact, at this point, you can try out the label field with our application.

Trying Out the Label Field

In The UiFunMainScreen constructor, replace this line:

```
add(new LabelField("Please enter your credentials:"));
```

with this one:

```
add(new CustomLabelField
    ("Please enter your credentials:", Color.WHITE, 0x999966, 0));
```

And the application will have a label with a different foreground and background (0x999966 is kind of a dark tan color), as shown in Figure 5-5.

Figure 5-5. *Using our custom label*

Adding an Image

Now, we'll add the ability to display an image to the left of the text. We'll create another constructor with a `Bitmap` parameter, and if this is specified, the `Bitmap` will be drawn at the left edge of the field, and the text will be shifted over to accommodate it. Let's start with the additional member variable and the constructor:

```
public class CustomLabelField extends Field {
    private Bitmap image;
    private String label;
    private int foregroundColor;
    private int backgroundColor;

    public CustomLabelField(String label, int foregroundColor,
            int backgroundColor, Bitmap image, long style) {
        super(style);
        this.label = label;
        this.foregroundColor = foregroundColor;
        this.backgroundColor = backgroundColor;
        this.image = image;
    }
}
```

We'll make a small change to the layout method, to handle the case where the image is taller than the font:

```
protected void layout(int width, int height) {
    if (image != null) {
        setExtent(width, Math.max(image.getHeight(), getFont().getHeight()));
    }
```

```
        else {
            setExtent(width, getFont().getHeight());
        }
    }
}
```

And we'll need to make another small change to the paint method. If we were given a bitmap, we'll draw it and set the x parameter to drawText to the right of the bitmap. We're also doing something else here: If the bitmap is taller than the font, we want the text centered vertically. Similarly, if the font is taller, we want the bitmap centered vertically. The algorithm in both cases is the same:

```
position = (Field height - item height) / 2
```

That's a good one to keep at hand; you'll end up using it often in your user interfaces (or the equivalent for horizontal centering).

Our new paint method looks like this:

```
    protected void paint(Graphics graphics) {
        graphics.setBackgroundColor(backgroundColor);
        graphics.clear();
        graphics.setColor(foregroundColor);
        if (image != null) {
            int textY = (getHeight() - getFont().getHeight()) / 2;
            int imageY = (getHeight() - image.getHeight()) / 2;
            graphics.drawBitmap(0, imageY, image.getWidth(), image.getHeight(),
                    image, 0, 0);
            graphics.drawText(label, image.getWidth(), textY);
        }
        else {
            graphics.drawText(label, 0, 0);
        }
    }
```

Graphics.drawBitmap is another good method to get familiar with. Its parameters let you draw part of a bitmap or a full bitmap, and it automatically takes into account image transparency, as you'll see when we put this new field to use with a partially transparent image.

Trying the new CustomLabelField

We'll change UiFunMainScreen's constructor again to use CustomLabelField's new constructor. We'll have to add a line to load the bitmap first, and add that bitmap to the project as before. You can get the image we're using here from this book's page web site.

The new lines for the constructor follow:

```
        Bitmap loginImage = Bitmap.getBitmapResource("res/login_arrow.png");
        add(new CustomLabelField
            ("Please enter your credentials:", Color.WHITE, 0x999966, loginImage, 0));
```

And running the application, you'll see the image and text together, as illustrated in Figure 5-6.

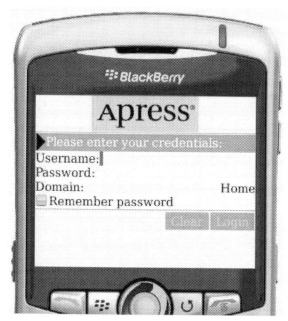

Figure 5-6. *The label showing our image*

Tying Up Some Loose Ends

The field works now, and in the end, when you're building a field for your application, all that matters is that it works where you want it to work. We'll fill in a couple of details here though, to make our CustomLabelField truly complete, and to illustrate a few additional concepts.

First, there are two methods which you *should* override but don't absolutely *have* to: getPreferredWidth and getPreferredHeight. These are used by some layout managers to help with determining field layout before a given field has had a chance to lay itself out. They let the manager know how much space the field needs ideally. There's no guarantee the manager will give the field that much space, or even call the methods, but they're easy to implement for our field, so for completeness, we'll implement them. getPreferredHeight is just the same algorithm we used in layout:

```
public int getPreferredHeight() {
    if (image != null) {
        return Math.max(getFont().getHeight(), image.getHeight());
    }
    else {
        return getFont().getHeight();
    }
}
```

The getPreferredWidth method is a bit trickier. Since we don't know the width available, we'll have to come up with a sensible value; in this case, we'll use the total width of the text in the field's font, plus the width of the image (if any):

```
public int getPreferredWidth() {
    int width = getFont().getAdvance(label);
    if (image != null) {
        width += image.getWidth();
    }
    return width;
}
```

The Font.getAdvance method just tells us the width, in pixels, needed to render the given string in that font.

Now, we'll take another look at layout. Two parameters were passed in, but we ignored the height parameter. What if the available height is less than the height we need for the font or image? It turns out the BlackBerry API will let us set a height that's bigger than the available height but will clip our field when it's drawn. Basically our paint method would think it had more space than it actually did, which would definitely lead to some drawing bugs. Given our field and application, it's unlikely we'll ever actually run into problems with the available height, but it does come into play with other fields, so let's modify our layout method to respect the height parameter. We'll also take this opportunity to eliminate some code replication. Since getPreferredHeight used exactly the same algorithm as layout, we'll just called getPreferredHeight, and if the height passed to layout is less than that, we'll cap the size at the smaller height:

```
protected void layout(int width, int height) {
    setExtent(width, Math.min(height, getPreferredHeight()));
}
```

Finally, what if our text is wider than the available width? This isn't unlikely; with a slightly larger font, wider image, or narrower screen, we could run out of room easily. Right now, the text will just cut off wherever the screen ends, even in the middle of a letter. Without getting into anything fancy, like text wrapping, we can use another version of Graphics.drawText that allows us to specify the width available for the text and set a flag to draw an ellipsis (. . .) at the end of our text if it exceeds the given space:

```
protected void paint(Graphics graphics) {
    graphics.setBackgroundColor(backgroundColor);
    graphics.clear();
    graphics.setColor(foregroundColor);
    if (image != null) {
        int textY = (getHeight() - getFont().getHeight()) / 2;
        int imageY = (getHeight() - image.getHeight()) / 2;
        graphics.drawBitmap(0, imageY, image.getWidth(), image.getHeight(),
                image, 0, 0);
        graphics.drawText(label, image.getWidth(), textY, DrawStyle.ELLIPSIS,
                getWidth()-image.getWidth());
    }
    else {
        graphics.drawText(label, 0, 0, DrawStyle.ELLIPSIS, getWidth());
    }
}
```

Now, if our label is too long, at least it'll look a bit better (see Figure 5-7).

Figure 5-7. *The CustomLabelField demonstrating the ellipsis*

Finally, let's revisit the layout method briefly. We made the field always take up the entire width available to it. What if we didn't want that behavior? How would the application using the field specify its behavior? Take a look at the field style flags available in the Field class. There's one called USE_ALL_WIDTH. Let's alter layout so that our label field only uses the full with of the screen if this flag is specified.

The change is simple:

```
protected void layout(int width, int height) {
    if ((getStyle() & Field.USE_ALL_WIDTH) == Field.USE_ALL_WIDTH) {
        setExtent(width, Math.min(height, getPreferredHeight()));
    }
    else {
        setExtent(getPreferredWidth(), getPreferredHeight());
    }
}
```

Again, we can use getPreferredWidth, because it already gives us the width of the image (if any) plus the text.

Finally, to make sure the label on our login screen still spans the entire width, we'll make a slight change to UiFunMainScreen's constructor, to pass in Field. USE_ALL_WIDTH as the style flag:

```
Add(new CustomLabelField
        ("Please enter your credentials:", Color.WHITF, 0x999966, loginImage,
Field.USE_ALL_WIDTH));
```

Congratulations, you've created your first custom field! You can take the appearance as far as you want (exploring the Graphics class may give you some ideas), but you understand the basics of building a field, except for one crucial piece: how to interact with the user. To illustrate *that*, we'll replace our application's buttons with something a bit different and learn how to create fields that a user can interact with.

Creating a Custom Button Field

To create our new buttons, we'll again start from scratch. Because you just worked through the basics of drawing a field, we'll focus only on areas that are different when creating an interactive field.

Laying Out the Interface

We'll start with the parts that you already know—the layout and paint methods. In this case, we want a size that's a bit bigger than our text, because we're going to draw a background for the button that extends beyond the text by a few pixels.

We also want to leave one pixel of blank space around the outside of the button, so the two buttons appear well spaced when they're next to each other on the screen. Figure 5-8 illustrates the horizontal sizing of the button relative to the text; the vertical layout is similar.

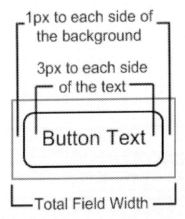

Figure 5-8. *The horizontal dimensions of the custom button field*

So, for the layout method, we just add 8 pixels (4 on each side) to the font advance for our button's text, and add 8 to the font height to get the field's size. Create a new class called CustomButtonField; the initial code should look like the following:

```
package com.beginningblackberry.uifun;

import net.rim.device.api.ui.Color;
import net.rim.device.api.ui.Field;
```

```
import net.rim.device.api.ui.Graphics;
import net.rim.device.api.ui.Keypad;

public class CustomButtonField extends Field {
    private String label;
    private int backgroundColor;
    private int foregroundColor;

    public CustomButtonField(String label, int foregroundColor,
            int backgroundColor, long style) {
        super(style);
        this.label = label;
        this.foregroundColor = foregroundColor;
        this.backgroundColor = backgroundColor;
    }

    public int getPreferredHeight() {
        return getFont().getHeight() + 8;
    }

    public int getPreferredWidth() {
        return getFont().getAdvance(label) + 8;
    }

    protected void layout(int width, int height) {
        setExtent
            (Math.min(width, getPreferredWidth()), Math.min(height,
getPreferredHeight()));
    }
}
```

Painting the Buttons

Instead of clearing the whole field to the background color, we'll just draw a rounded rectangle of the given background color, and draw the text on top of that. We'll have to come back to paint when we make this field focusable, but for now, to get something on screen, our paint method looks like this:

```
protected void paint(Graphics graphics) {
    graphics.setColor(backgroundColor);
    graphics.fillRoundRect(1, 1, getWidth()-2, getHeight()-2, 12, 12);
    graphics.setColor(foregroundColor);
    graphics.drawText(label, 4, 4);
}
```

Taking a Look

Replace the ButtonFields in UiFunMainScreen with CustomButtonFields, and you'll see how the buttons look so far. In UiFunMainScreen's constructor, change the class for the button declarations from ButtonField to CustomButtonField:

```
CustomButtonField clearButton;
CustomButtonField loginButton;
```

Then, in UiFunMainScreen's constructor replace the following lines:

```
clearButton = new ButtonField("Clear", ButtonField.CONSUME_CLICK);
clearButton.setChangeListener(this);
loginButton = new ButtonField("Login", ButtonField.CONSUME_CLICK);
loginButton.setChangeListener(this);
```

with these lines:

```
clearButton = new CustomButtonField("Clear", Color.WHITE, Color.LIGHTGREY, 0);
clearButton.setChangeListener(this);
loginButton = new CustomButtonField("Login", Color.WHITE, Color.LIGHTGREY, 0);
loginButton.setChangeListener(this);
```

Running the application, you'll see, as you should expect by now, our buttons drawn to the screen as illustrated in Figure 5-9.

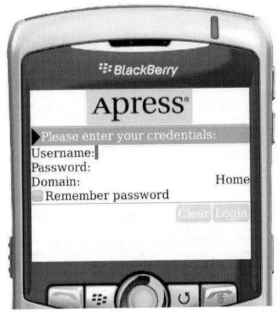

Figure 5-9. *Two buttons, rounded rectangles with text – no surprises*

If you try to use the application now, however, you'll notice a big difference; you can no longer select the buttons!

Making the Button Focusable

Because most BlackBerry devices use a trackball as their navigation method, the concept of *focus* is very important. The field with focus is the one that receives events from the user interface and has the first chance to respond to them. (Even the BlackBerry Storm preserves the notion of focus, though having focus is not as critical. When you lightly tap the screen on top of a field, it receives focus.)

To make the button focusable we'll just override isFocusable in CustomButtonField to return true:

```
public boolean isFocusable() {
    return true;
}
```

Now, you'll be able to move the focus down to the buttons, but the visual representation shown in Figure 5-10 is not what we want.

Figure 5-10. *Custom button fields with the default focus drawing behavior*

Drawing the Focus

The default focus behavior for the BlackBerry is to invert pixels that are in the background color. This look is fine for many types of fields, but for our button field, we want to change the button to a color that the user specifies at instantiation time.

First, let's add a couple of member variables, so we can specify the color of the focused button's text and background:

```
private int focusedForegroundColor;
private int focusedBackgroundColor;

public CustomButtonField(String label, int foregroundColor,
        int backgroundColor, int focusedForegroundColor,
        int focusedBackgroundColor, long style) {
    super(style);
    this.label = label;
    this.foregroundColor = foregroundColor;
    this.backgroundColor = backgroundColor;
    this.focusedForegroundColor = focusedForegroundColor;
```

```
        this.focusedBackgroundColor = focusedBackgroundColor;
    }
```

Now, we'll disable the default focus behavior so that blue rectangle isn't drawn. To do this, we just override drawFocus and have it do nothing:

```
    protected void drawFocus(Graphics graphics, boolean on) {
    }
```

Field has a method called isFocus that lets us determine if the field is in focus while we're painting. We'll make use of this in our paint method to draw the button in different colors when it's in focus. To illustrate a little bit more about drawing using the Graphics object, we're also going to add a shine effect to our focused button by drawing a semitransparent white rounded rectangle on top of the button background:

```
    protected void paint(Graphics graphics) {
        if (isFocus()) {
            graphics.setColor(focusedBackgroundColor);
            graphics.fillRoundRect(1, 1, getWidth()-2, getHeight()-2, 12, 12);
            graphics.setColor(Color.WHITE);
            graphics.setGlobalAlpha(100);
            graphics.fillRoundRect(3, 3, getWidth()-6, getHeight()/2, 12, 12);
            graphics.setGlobalAlpha(255);
            graphics.setColor(focusedForegroundColor);
            graphics.drawText(label, 4, 4);
        }
        else {
            graphics.setColor(backgroundColor);
            graphics.fillRoundRect(1, 1, getWidth()-2, getHeight()-2, 12, 12);
            graphics.setColor(foregroundColor);
            graphics.drawText(label, 4, 4);
        }
    }
```

Transparency is specified through the setGlobalAlpha method on the graphics object. It takes an int that can range from 0 for fully transparent to 255 for fully opaque and affects all subsequent drawing operations with that Graphics object, so be sure to reset the alpha value to 255 before the end of your paint method, or you may see some strange effects in your application.

Finally, we need to have the button repaint when its focus state changes. This does not happen automatically, so we need to override onFocus and onUnfocus to explicitly invalidate the field. Be sure to call the superclass's versions of these methods to maintain the focus behavior:

```
    protected void onFocus(int direction) {
        super.onFocus(direction);
        invalidate();
    }

    protected void onUnfocus() {
        super.onUnfocus();
        invalidate();
    }
```

Changing the button initialization in UiFunMainScreen's constructor, we'll specify a green and yellow color scheme for our buttons they have focus:

```
clearButton = new CustomButtonField
    ("Clear", Color.WHITE, Color.LIGHTGREY, Color.YELLOW, Color.GREEN, 0);
clearButton.setChangeListener(this);
loginButton = new CustomButtonField
    ("Login", Color.WHITE, Color.LIGHTGREY, Color.YELLOW, Color.GREEN, 0);
loginButton.setChangeListener(this);
```

Now, everything will look a lot better (see Figure 5-11).

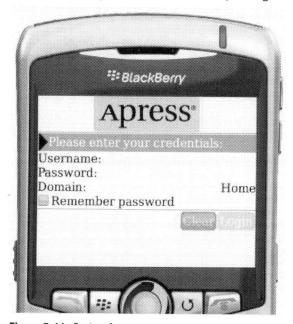

Figure 5-11. *Custom focus appearance*

Now, we have buttons that look as we want them to when focused, but when we click them, nothing happens. The final piece to put in place is to have each trackball or touch screen click fire a field-changed event.

Handling Events

Fortunately, the API makes event handling very easy. All we have to do is override navigationClick and call fieldChangeNotify. The API takes care of handling the listener and calling its fieldChanged method:

```
protected boolean navigationClick(int status, int time) {
    fieldChangeNotify(0);
    return true;
}
```

The status parameter is unimportant for our purposes, but comparing it against values defined in net.rim.device.api.system.KeypadListener would let us determine if the Alt, Shift, or other keys were being pressed while the user clicked our field.

Returning true from this method lets the framework know that we handled this event, so no one else should respond to it.

Finally, the BlackBerry ButtonField also fires an event when the user presses the Enter key while the field has focus. We'll implement that behavior by overriding keyChar:

```
protected boolean keyChar(char character, int status, int time) {
    if (character == Keypad.KEY_ENTER) {
        fieldChangeNotify(0);
        return true;
    }
    return super.keyChar(character, status, time);
}
```

The Enter key is the only one this field should handle, so we fire a field changed event and return true if that's the case. Otherwise, we call the superclass's method that will allow other interested components to handle this keypress if they want.

Trying it out, we'll get the same results as with the BlackBerry ButtonField class, as shown in Figure 5-12.

Figure 5-12. *The fully functional CustomButtonField*

Now we've got a fully customized button field that acts like a built-in ButtonField.

A Review of Custom Fields

You can extend the concepts here to make your buttons include images, have different fonts, or anything else your application requires. The same concepts will also let you create many different types of fields.

Remember, when implementing a field from scratch you should be concerned with these methods:

- paint
- layout

And when creating an interactive field, you should override at least these methods as well:

- isFocusable
- onFocus
- onUnfocus
- drawFocus
- navigationClick
- keyChar

Creating Custom Managers

Now let's turn our attention to the username, password, and domain fields. We want the labels to line up to the right. To do that, we'll have to make two changes. The first is easy—we'll stop using the built-in labels of the EditFields and ObjectChoiceField and replace them with LabelFields. We'll use HorizontalFieldManagers as we do for the buttons to keep the labels and edit fields on the same line. The new code for the UiFunMainScreen constructor follows:

```
usernameField = new EditField("", "");
LabelField usernameLabel = new LabelField("Username:", Field.FIELD_RIGHT);
HorizontalFieldManager usernameManager = new HorizontalFieldManager();
usernameManager.add(usernameLabel);
usernameManager.add(usernameField);
passwordField = new PasswordEditField("", "");
LabelField passwordLabel = new LabelField("Password:", Field.FIELD_RIGHT);

HorizontalFieldManager passwordManager = new HorizontalFieldManager();
passwordManager.add(passwordLabel);
passwordManager.add(passwordField);
domainField = new ObjectChoiceField("", new String[] {"Home", "Work"});
LabelField domainLabel = new LabelField("Domain:", Field.FIELD_RIGHT);
HorizontalFieldManager domainManager = new HorizontalFieldManager();
domainManager.add(domainLabel);
domainManager.add(domainField);
```

```
add(usernameManager);
add(passwordManager);
add(domainManager);
```

We've given the labels the Field.FIELD_RIGHT style, which will be important later but doesn't affect the appearance because of the way the horizontal field managers function in this configuration. The appearance of the application is the same as before, but the horizontal field managers are outlined to clarify the discussion that will follow (see Figure 5-13).

Figure 5-13. *Separate labels and fields in horizontal field managers.*

One quick way to get the labels and fields to line up the way we want them is to create two vertical field managers, one for the labels and one for the fields. We can rely on the fact that the fields and labels are the same height to make them line up vertically. The two vertical field managers go inside one horizontal field manager, which is added to the screen. We're not going to pursue this, but for illustrative purposes Figure 5-14 shows how the screen looks, again with the managers outlined.

Figure 5-14. *Using VerticalFieldManagers to line up the components*

That looks pretty good. So what's the problem? We're relying on the fact that the label fields are the same height as the other fields. This is not guaranteed—a fact we can illustrate by typing in a long username as shown in Figure 5-15.

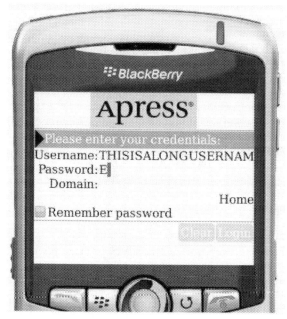

Figure 5-15. *Knocking the fields out of alignment*

What we really want is a grid of labels and fields. We'll do this by creating a grid field manager.

Creating a Manager

Managers are, in many ways, simpler to implement than fields. You're only required to implement one method, `sublayout`, and unless you're doing something really complex, the basic `net.rim.device.api.ui.Manager` paint method will still work and draw your fields wherever you positioned them.

Managers do have to be concerned with things like moving the focus from field to field, but if we're clever enough about things, we won't have to worry about handling that ourselves either. The functionality that `net.rim.device.api.ui.Manager` gives us will be enough.

Understanding GridFieldManager

`GridFieldManager` will let the user specify a number of grid columns when it's instantiated. The number of rows will vary depending on the number of fields added.

For a horizontal or vertical manager, it's clear where fields are positioned, either left to right or top to bottom in the order they're added (we'll ignore `insert` for now). For a grid manager, it's not as clear which way we should add them. Should they be added left to right, then top to bottom, or the other way around? So we'll just choose to go left to right and then top to bottom as shown in Figure 5-16

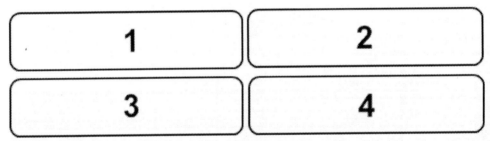

Figure 5-16. This is our field layout for the grid manager; the numbers represent the order the fields were added to the manager.

Implementing the Basic Framework

We'll subclass directly from net.rim.device.api.ui.Manager and build our Manager from scratch. The only thing we'll need to keep track of is the number of columns. The Manager class already maintains the list of fields for us:

```
package com.beginningblackberry.uifun;

import net.rim.device.api.ui.Field;
import net.rim.device.api.ui.Manager;
```

```
public class GridFieldManager extends Manager {
    private int numColumns;

    public GridFieldManager(int numColumns, long style) {
        super(style);
        this.numColumns = numColumns;
    }

    protected void sublayout(int width, int height) {
    }
}
```

Implementing the sublayout Method

All the magic in a manager happens in the sublayout method. It's similar to a field's layout method, down to the requirement that you call setExtent within the method to set the manager's size (and in fact, behind the scenes, the manager's layout method calls sublayout). Remember, a manager is ultimately a type of field.

The other requirement in a manager's sublayout method is that you position and size all the fields contained by the manager. This is done through the layoutChild and setPositionChild methods. The layoutChild method will result more or less directly in a call to the child field's layout method, meaning that before you call layoutChild the child field will return 0 from getWidth and getHeight.

Here's where we have to think about how exactly we'll determine how wide each column should be. In our case, we're using the manager in a limited fashion, and we control how it's used. Therefore, we can make some assumptions about the types of fields that will be contained; specifically, we can ensure that fields will in general all be able to fit in a row across the screen. When designing general-purpose managers, many of these design decisions can quickly become very complex; it's usually good practice to keep in mind where you're going to be using your manager and design to that, rather than attempting to design for the general case right away.

We'll also assume that we don't have to worry about having enough vertical space for the manager. In fact, if we end up in a constrained vertical space, the manager will just be cut off at the bottom, and it's not certain that we could really do much better than that.

So our manager's sublayout method will do the following:

1. Go through the fields in the first (leftmost) column and call layoutChild on each one, so get an accurate width and height.

2. Determine the width of the first column from the maximum width of all the fields.

3. Subtract that width from the total available, and continue to layout the fields in each column in turn, left to right.

4. Set the position for all fields in the first row based on the column widths.

5. Set the position for all fields in the second row based on the column widths and the maximum height of all the fields in the first row, and continue top to bottom for all the rows.

6. Set the extent of the field based on the total width of all columns and the total height of all rows.

Clear? Here's how all the code looks:

```
protected void sublayout(int width, int height) {
    int[] columnWidths = new int[numColumns];
    int availableWidth = width;
    int availableHeight = height;

    // For each column size all the fields and get the maximum width
    for(int column = 0; column < numColumns; column++) {
        for
        (int fieldIndex = column; fieldIndex < getFieldCount(); fieldIndex +=
numColumns){
            Field field = getField(fieldIndex);
            layoutChild(field, availableWidth, availableHeight);
            if (field.getWidth() > columnWidths[column]) {
                columnWidths[column] = field.getWidth();
            }

        }

        availableWidth -= columnWidths[column];
    }

    int currentRow = 0;
    int currentRowHeight = 0;
    int rowYOffset = 0;

    // Set the position of each field
    for(int fieldIndex = 0; fieldIndex < getFieldCount(); fieldIndex++) {
        Field field = getField(fieldIndex);
        if (fieldIndex % numColumns == 0) {
            setPositionChild(field, 0, rowYOffset);
        }
        else {
            setPositionChild
                (field, columnWidths[(fieldIndex % numColumns) - 1], rowYOffset);
        }

        if (field.getHeight() > currentRowHeight) {
            currentRowHeight = field.getHeight();
        }

        if (fieldIndex % numColumns == numColumns - 1) {
            currentRow ++;
            rowYOffset += currentRowHeight;
            currentRowHeight = 0;
```

```
        }
    }

    int totalWidth = 0;
    for(int i = 0; i < numColumns; i++) {
        totalWidth += columnWidths[i];
    }
    setExtent(totalWidth, rowYOffset + currentRowHeight);
}
```

There's a lot to this method, so let's walk through it. The first for loop iterates through all the fields in the manager, one column at a time and calls layoutChild on each one to set its size:

```
for(int column = 0; column < numColumns; column++) {
    for(int fieldIndex = column; fieldIndex < getFieldCount(); fieldIndex += numColumns) {
```

If we have a two-column grid with six fields, we go through the fields in this order (starting with 0):

```
Column 0:
    0
    2
    4
Column 1:
    1
    3
    5
```

For each column, we lay out all the fields in whatever width we have available, and then take the maximum width as the column width. We subtract that width from the total remaining width to get the available width for the next columns.

Once we've determined the column widths, the next for loop again goes through all the fields in the manager, to position them on screen using setPositionChild:

```
for(int fieldIndex = 0; fieldIndex < getFieldCount(); fieldIndex++) {
            Field field = getField(fieldIndex);
            if (fieldIndex % numColumns == 0) {
                setPositionChild(field, 0, rowYOffset);
            }
            else {
                setPositionChild
                    (field, columnWidths[(fieldIndex % numColumns) - 1], rowYOffset);
            }
```

We have the column widths already so we know where they should be positioned horizontally. As we lay out each row, we keep track of the field with the largest height in that row, and use that as the row height:

```
            if (field.getHeight() > currentRowHeight) {
                currentRowHeight = field.getHeight();
            }
```

When we're at the last field of a row (where the index is one less than a multiple of the number of columns), we shift the vertical position for the next row downward, and start over again:

```
    if (fieldIndex % numColumns == numColumns - 1) {
        currentRow ++;
        rowYOffset += currentRowHeight;
        currentRowHeight = 0;
    }
```

Finally, we set the size for the manager by adding up all the column widths, and taking the total of all the row heights:

```
int totalWidth = 0;
for(int i = 0; i < numColumns; i++) {
    totalWidth += columnWidths[i];
}
setExtent(totalWidth, rowYOffset + currentRowHeight);
```

Seeing the Grid Field Manager in Action

OK, now let's see how the grid looks. We'll modify UiFunMainScreen's constructor again to use the grid field manager to hold our separate labels and edit fields:

```
usernameField = new EditField("", "");
LabelField usernameLabel = new LabelField("Username:", Field.FIELD_RIGHT);
passwordField = new PasswordEditField("", "");
LabelField passwordLabel = new LabelField("Password:", Field.FIELD_RIGHT);

domainField = new ObjectChoiceField("", new String[] {"Home", "Work"});
LabelField domainLabel = new LabelField("Domain:", Field.FIELD_RIGHT);

GridFieldManager gridFieldManager = new GridFieldManager(2, 0);
gridFieldManager.add(usernameLabel);
gridFieldManager.add(usernameField);
gridFieldManager.add(passwordLabel);
gridFieldManager.add(passwordField);
gridFieldManager.add(domainLabel);
gridFieldManager.add(domainField);

add(gridFieldManager);
```

Remember, because we've instantiated a two-column grid, the labels will all appear in the left column and the edit fields on the right.

Now, start the simulator, and you should see something like Figure 5-17.

Figure 5-17. *Using the first version of the grid field manager*

We're doing better already. The username can wrap, and all the labels stay aligned with the field. Incidentally if you're paying attention, you might realize that when the text in the username field wraps, it causes the screen's layout method to be run again. This behavior is fine and expected: layout happens infrequently, but it does happen.

Aligning the Labels

There's one problem though. While the edit fields are aligned properly, the labels are still aligned to the left, rather than the right, despite the fact that we gave them the Field.FIELD_RIGHT styles. Remember earlier that I mentioned that styles were dependent on the field and the manager? Our GridFieldManager has to explicitly support the FIELD_RIGHT style to get the alignment to work the way we expect it to. The change is simple. If the field has the FIELD_RIGHT style set, we just need to shift it to the right by the width of the column minus the width of the field. In sublayout replace the following lines:

```
if (fieldIndex % numColumns == 0) {
    setPositionChild(field, 0, rowYOffset);
}
else {
    setPositionChild
        (field, columnWidths[(fieldIndex % numColumns) - 1], rowYOffset);
}
```

with these:

```
int fieldOffset = 0;
```

```
        if ((field.getStyle() & Field.FIELD_RIGHT) == Field.FIELD_RIGHT) {
            fieldOffset = columnWidths[fieldIndex % numColumns] - field.getWidth();
        }
        if (fieldIndex % numColumns == 0) {
            setPositionChild(field, 0 + fieldOffset, rowYOffset);
        }
        else {
            setPositionChild
                (field, columnWidths[(fieldIndex % numColumns) - 1] + fieldOffset,
rowYOffset);
        }
```

Now, our manager positions all of the label fields correctly (see Figure 5-18).

Figure 5-18. *The labels are aligned on the right. Notice that wrapping is supported for the password field too.*

If you wanted to support Field.FIELD_HCENTER, the change would be similar. I'll leave that as an exercise for you.

Focus Movement

If you play with this application, you'll notice that the focus moves as you'd expect it to: when the cursor is in the username field, scrolling down or right will move the cursor to the password field and then to the domain drop-down. This is because of the default focus movement behavior, which is to use the order the fields are added to the manager as the focus order and to move to later fields in the focus order when the trackball is moved right or down and to earlier fields when the trackball is moved left or up.

This behavior wouldn't work if we had more than one column of focusable fields in our manager. Imagine we have two columns of focusable fields. Figures 5-19 through 5-22 illustrate the focus movement problems. The numbers represent the order fields are added to the grid field manager.

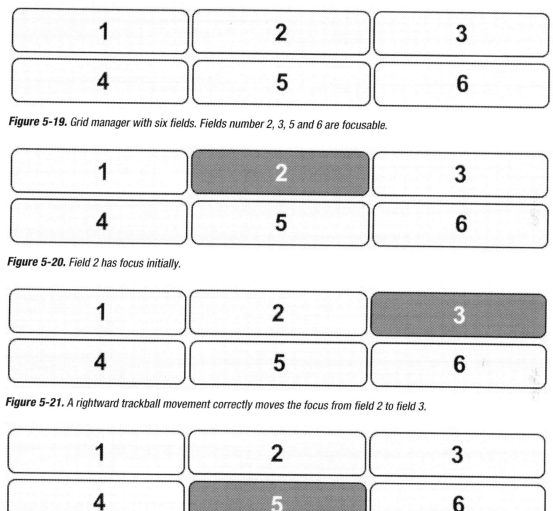

Figure 5-19. Grid manager with six fields. Fields number 2, 3, 5 and 6 are focusable.

Figure 5-20. Field 2 has focus initially.

Figure 5-21. A rightward trackball movement correctly moves the focus from field 2 to field 3.

Figure 5-22. A downward trackball movement moves the focus from field 3 to field 5, which is not the behavior we expect.

This problem exists because the default focus-moving algorithm doesn't take into account field position on the screen, only field order within the manager. So moving right and down are considered to be the same action. You can fix this by overriding navigationMovement in your manager, but the discussion about how to do so is beyond the scope of this book. The source code available on the book's web site includes a sample implementation for moving focus in a grid field.

Tidying Up the Login Success Screen

Now that we've got a few components, let's revisit LoginSuccessScreen. With some simple modifications to the constructor to use our CustomLabelField and GridFieldManager, we can make the screen look a little better.

```
public LoginSuccessScreen(String username, String domain) {
    try {
        FontFamily alphaSansFamily = FontFamily.forName("BBAlpha Serif");
        Font appFont = alphaSansFamily.getFont(Font.PLAIN, 9, Ui.UNITS_pt);
        setFont(appFont);
    } catch (ClassNotFoundException e) {
    }

    add(new CustomLabelField("Logged In!", Color.WHITE, 0x999966,
Field.USE_ALL_WIDTH));
    add(new SeparatorField());
    GridFieldManager gridFieldManager = new GridFieldManager(2, 0);
    gridFieldManager.add
        (new CustomLabelField("Username:", Color.BLACK, Color.WHITE,
Field.FIELD_RIGHT));
    gridFieldManager.add
        (new CustomLabelField(username, Color.BLACK, Color.LIGHTGREY,
Field.USE_ALL_WIDTH));
    gridFieldManager.add
        (new CustomLabelField("Domain:", Color.BLACK, Color.WHITE,
Field.FIELD_RIGHT));
    gridFieldManager.add
        (new CustomLabelField(domain, Color.BLACK, Color.LIGHTGREY,
Field.USE_ALL_WIDTH));
    add(gridFieldManager);
}
```

Here, we've moved the username and domain labels and values into a grid, similar to our main screen. Notice that we've given the right column labels the Field.USE_ALL_WIDTH value, which, in combination with the sublayout method of the grid field manager, will make them use the entire screen width except for the space taken by the first column. Go back and see if you can figure out why, and try to figure out what would happen if we applied Field.USE_ALL_WIDTH to the labels for the *first* column.

The screen with the constructor provided in this section will look something like Figure 5-23.

Figure 5-23. *The redone login success screen*

Now, you should be familiar with how to make fields and managers. That leaves one more piece of the visual BlackBerry user interface to cover before we're finished this chapter—screens.

Creating a Custom Screen

We're actually using three screens in our UI Fun application already. Two are obvious: UiFunMainScreen and the login success screen. The third is the dialog that appears when you try to log in without entering a username and password (see Figure 5-24).

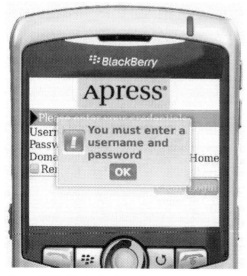

Figure 5-24. *The login dialog is a Screen too*

A screen on the BlackBerry doesn't have to take up the entire display; other screens can be visible below it. All screens, however, do take over the user input. That is, any keypresses, trackball presses, or touch screen taps only go to whatever screen is currently active and on top of the display stack. The active screen is also the one that controls the menu.

All screens are derived from net.rim.device.api.ui.Screen. We'll illustrate the concepts by creating a custom dialog to replace the default one, if for no other reason than we want to use our own colors and font and replace the OK button with one of our custom button fields.

We'll name our new screen CustomDialog (you should be seeing a pattern in our names by now) and directly subclass Screen. There is a PopupScreen class in net.rim.device.api.ui.container, but it adds some things that we don't want, like a border. The basic code looks like this:

```
package com.beginningblackberry.uifun;

import net.rim.device.api.ui.Screen;
import net.rim.device.api.ui.container.VerticalFieldManager;

public class CustomDialog extends Screen {
    public CustomDialog(String message) {
        super(new VerticalFieldManager());
    }

    protected void sublayout(int width, int height) {
    }
}
```

Right away, you should notice two things. First, we're required to implement sublayout; this will actually be much easier than with a manager. Second, we're required to pass a Manager to Screen's constructor. This is the delegate manager.

Delegate Managers

A screen doesn't directly lay out any of its fields. Instead, it delegates that to a manager that's specified when the screen is instantiated. All the manager methods on the screen (add, delete, insert, etc.) actually end up invoking the same methods on the delegate manager. The only component the screen handles directly is the delegate manager. This separation of manager and screen makes it easy to change the internal layout of any screen. This also means that a screen must have a delegate manager at all times, so it must be specified at instantiation time and can never be changed. The delegate manager can be any valid Manager class, as there are no extra requirements above what a regular Manager does.

Implementing the Screen's sublayout Method

As we've discussed, the screen's sublayout method needs to worry about only the delegate manager. This is accessible through the getDelegate method. There are a couple of special methods in Screen that allow us to layout the delegate manager and position it. These methods work the same as the methods to set field position and size in any other manager. In addition to this, our sublayout method needs to set the extent of the screen, just as with any field, and set the position of the screen on the display. The width and height parameters passed into the sublayout method of a screen will always be the width and height of the device's display (on a device with a rotatable display, like the BlackBerry Storm, these will represent the current orientation of the screen).

Note that setPosition sets the position of the screen relative to the device's display; that is, setPosition(10, 10) will position the screen 10 pixels from the top-left corner of the display. setPositionDelegate sets the position of the delegate manager relative to the screen's position.

We're going to give the delegate manager slightly less room than is available to us, to ensure the screen's contents don't take up the entire screen and to leave room for us to draw a border around the screen. When we've determined the size of the delegate, we set the actual size of the screen accordingly:

```
protected void sublayout(int width, int height) {
    layoutDelegate(width - 80, height - 80);
    setPositionDelegate(10, 10);
    setExtent(width - 60, Math.min(height - 60, getDelegate().getHeight() + 20));
    setPosition(30, (height - getHeight())/2);
}
```

We're leaving 30 pixels to the left and right of the screen and a minimum of 30 to the top and bottom, though if the delegate is small, we'll have more space. We're also leaving a 10-pixel border on all sides between the edges of the screen and the edges of the delegate manager to give us space to draw our border.

Let's add a LabelField to the constructor and make a change in UiFunMainScreen to see this in action. First, edit CustomDialog's constructor:

```
public CustomDialog(String message) {
    super(new VerticalFieldManager(), Screen.DEFAULT_CLOSE);
    add(new LabelField(message));
}
```

The add method here actually delegates to the VerticalFieldManager constructed on the preceding line. Also, we've added the Screen.DEFAULT_CLOSE style so that pressing the escape button will close this screen.

In UiFunMainScreen, modify the login method by replacing the line that shows the dialog:

```
Dialog.alert("You must enter a username and password");
```

with the following line to instantiate and show our custom dialog:

```
UiApplication.getUiApplication().pushModalScreen
    (new CustomDialog("You must enter a username and password"));
```

Now, run the application, and click the Login button (or menu item), and you'll see a basic screen like the one in Figure 5-25.

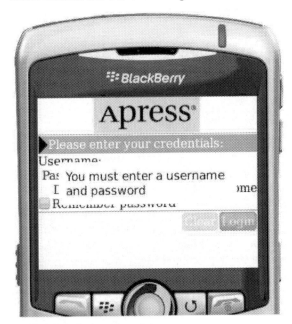

Figure 5-25. *Basic custom dialog*

Right now, there's not much too it, just a white square with our LabelField on it, but it is a screen. Try typing, and you'll notice that the rest of the application doesn't respond. The custom dialog is intercepting all the keypresses. Pressing the escape key will dismiss the dialog.

Adding a Few Fields

We'll modify the constructor to add an OK button and a separator field to fill out the dialog. We'll also set the font while we're at it. The following is the new constructor:

```
public CustomDialog(String message) {
    super(new VerticalFieldManager(), Screen.DEFAULT_CLOSE);
    try {
        FontFamily alphaSansFamily = FontFamily.forName("BBAlpha Serif");
        Font appFont = alphaSansFamily.getFont(Font.PLAIN, 9, Ui.UNITS_pt);
        setFont(appFont);
    } catch (ClassNotFoundException e) {
    }

    add(new LabelField(message));

    add(new SeparatorField());
```

```
    okButton = new CustomButtonField
    ("OK", Color.WHITE, Color.LIGHTGREY, Color.YELLOW, Color.GREEN,
Field.FIELD_HCENTER);
    okButton.setChangeListener(this);
    add(okButton);
}
```

We're using the same color scheme for the OK button as with the buttons on UiFunMainScreen. We'll also have to make CustomDialog implement FieldChangeListener and provide an appropriate fieldChanged method:

```
public class CustomDialog extends Screen implements FieldChangeListener {
    private CustomButtonField okButton;

    //...

    public void fieldChanged(Field field, int context) {
        if (field == okButton) {
            close();
        }
    }
}
```

Painting the Background

Just to illustrate the concept, we'll draw a simple background consisting of a rounded rectangle in our tan color outlined in black. The paintBackground method is the place to do this; we won't interfere with painting of the fields which is already handled just fine by the Screen class:

```
protected void paintBackground(Graphics graphics) {
    graphics.setColor(0x999966);
    graphics.fillRoundRect(0, 0, getWidth(), getHeight(), 12, 12);
    graphics.setColor(Color.BLACK);
    graphics.drawRoundRect(0, 0, getWidth(), getHeight(), 12, 12);
}
```

Now, let's run the application again and take a look at our completed dialog (see Figure 5-26).

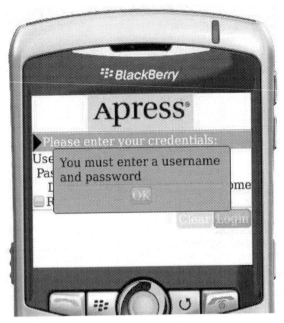

Figure 5-26. *The completed custom dialog*

The border between the outside edge of the screen and the delegate manager is now apparent by looking at the label and separator fields. Clicking OK will close the dialog, as we'd expect.

Adding the Final Touches

We're almost there. All that's left is to change the color of the background behind the logo image and make a couple of minor tweaks to alignment. I've left this section until almost the end of this chapter, because there's not a lot new here; we're just applying concepts that you already know.

Adding a Header Background

We want to put a black background behind the header image and align the image to the left. The second change is easy; simply change the style Field.FIELD_HCENTER to Field.FIELD_LEFT (or leave it out entirely, as FIELD_LEFT is the default).

To make the image sit on a different color background, we'll put the BitmapField inside another manager and let that manager draw the background color. We'll use a HorizontalFieldManager. This first part should be familiar to you by now. Change the following lines in the UiFunMainScreen constructor:

```
Bitmap logoBitmap = Bitmap.getBitmapResource("res/apress_logo.png");
bitmapField = new BitmapField(logoBitmap, Field.FIELD_LEFT);
```

```
        HorizontalFieldManager hfmLabel = new
HorizontalFieldManager(Field.USE_ALL_WIDTH);
        hfmLabel.add(bitmapField);
        add(hfmLabel);
```

The background is still white, but we've set the stage to change it. Now, there are two ways we can go about providing a black background. Before version 4.6 of the operating system, we would have to subclass the HorizontalFieldManager and modify the paint method. In version 4.6, RIM introduced a new method. We'll cover both methods briefly.

Subclassing HorizontalFieldManager

There's a simple Java construct called an anonymous inner class that lets us define a class at the same time as we instantiate it, if we need only one instance of the new class, as we do here. I'll present the code and discuss it afterward. Replace the new HorizontalFieldManager line with the following lines:

```
        HorizontalFieldManager hfmLabel = new
HorizontalFieldManager(Field.USE_ALL_WIDTH) {
            protected void paint(Graphics graphics) {
                graphics.setBackgroundColor(Color.BLACK);
                graphics.clear();
                super.paint(graphics);
            }
        };
```

This code redefines the paint method only for this instance of HorizontalFieldManager. The new paint method is simple. It just clears the entire background of the manager to black and then calls super.paint to draw the rest of the manager as before.

Using Background and BackgroundFactory

The version 4.6 of the JDE and operating system introduced borders and backgrounds, which can be used to modify the appearance of UI components. For this to work, you have to use JDE 4.6 or later, or configure the Eclipse Plug-in to use the JDE component pack 4.6 or later.

The border and background classes can be found in the net.rim.device.api.ui.decor package. We're interested in BackgroundFactory and Background. The code is pretty self-explanatory—we create a solid black background, and attach it to our HorizontalFieldManager:

```
        HorizontalFieldManager hfmLabel = new
HorizontalFieldManager(Field.USE_ALL_WIDTH);
        Background blackBackground =
BackgroundFactory.createSolidBackground(Color.BLACK);
        hfmLabel.setBackground(blackBackground);
```

Both the subclass method and the background method produce the same result, which is shown in Figure 5-27.

Figure 5-27. *A black background for our image*

Which method should you use to set the background color? For now, I recommend subclassing `HorizontalFieldManager`, because it works with versions of the operating system before 4.5, and a lot of devices out there are still running those operating systems. If you use `BackgroundFactory` and `Background`, your application will not run on devices with version 4.5 or older. In the future though, expect this to change. Think of this as a sneak preview of the way BlackBerry development will be done in the near future.

Making Minor Tweaks

Just to complete the look we wanted, we'll do a couple of small things. First, we want the labels to be indented from the left side a bit—we'll accomplish that just by adding a few spaces to the beginning of the Username label—since everything is in a grid layout, the other fields will still line up with the right side of the label:

```
LabelField usernameLabel = new LabelField("   Username:", Field.FIELD_RIGHT);
```

Finally, let's align the Remember password check box to the right. Just add the `Field.FIELD_RIGHT` alignment style to it:

```
        rememberCheckbox = new CheckboxField("Remember password", false,
Field.FIELD_RIGHT);
```

Now, our main screen is exactly as we wanted to see it, as illustrated in Figure 5-28.

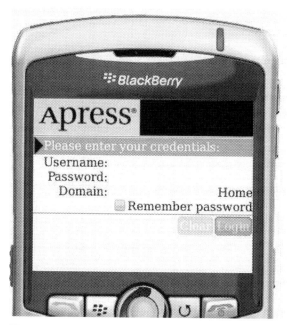

Figure 5-28. *The finished UiFun main screen*

Working with the BlackBerry Storm

In most of the work we've done so far, I've mentioned the trackball many times, as most BlackBerry devices are trackball (or trackpad) devices after all. But what about the BlackBerry Storm with its touch screen?

The good news is that, if you construct your components the way we've done here, everything will work as you'd expect on the Storm. The BlackBerry operating system maps touch events to appropriate focus or navigation click events on your screens and fields, so as long as you're working at the level of those methods, you don't have to do any extra work to be compatible with the touch screen input method. You will, as discussed earlier, have to compile your code with JDE 4.7 or later to avoid compatibility mode, but the code itself won't have to change.

The other new feature of the Storm is that you can use it in vertical and horizontal orientation. The good news is that, since we've used relative positioning everywhere, our application will look good automatically on the Storm in both vertical and horizontal orientation (see Figures 5-29 and 5-30).

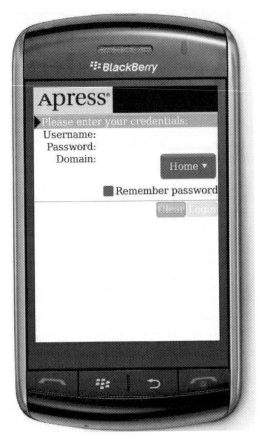

Figure 5-29. *UiFun running on the BlackBerry Storm simulator in vertical orientation*

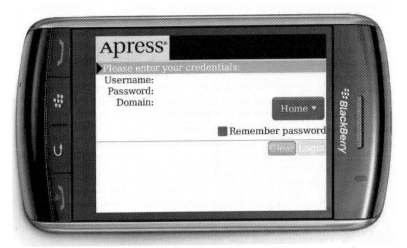

Figure 5-30. *UiFun running on the BlackBerry Storm simulator in a horizontal orientation*

When the device is rotated, your `sublayout` and `layout` methods will automatically be called, and you'll have a chance to adjust your screen layout to the new width and height.

The virtual keyboard will also automatically be displayed whenever the focus is on a text edit field.

Creating Basic Animation

We're going to spend a little bit of time on a topic that can really make your user interface shine—animation. Now, this topic is more advanced, and really only recently have applications with fancier screen transitions and other effects started to appear. So you're fine without animation. This section will teach you a bit more about how the BlackBerry UI API works though, and it's kind of fun, so I recommend you at least read through it.

The BlackBerry platform, at the time of this writing, doesn't offer any transitions between screens by default. In our application, when you click the Login button, the login screen instantly appears; it doesn't fade in, slide in, or anything like that. We'll modify `UiFun` so that when the user logs in (clicks the Login button after typing a username and password), the login success screen slides up from the bottom of the display.

The basic idea for user interface animation is to pick an aspect of the user interface to animate (size, position, transparency) and a time for the animation to take place (for example, 300 milliseconds for a screen to slide onto the display). Then, in each update of the user interface, check if the animation time has elapsed: if not, update the user interface aspect according to how much time has passed, and queue up another UI update.

Using time-based animation like this means that the animation will run as smoothly as possible across different device models and under different conditions and will always take the same amount of time to complete.

Setting the Vertical Offset

To get the animation started, add a new variable to `LoginSuccessScreen` called `verticalOffset`:

```
private int verticalOffset;
```

We'll update this variable during the animation, decrementing it from the display height to zero.

We'll also add another variable and a constant `final` variable to keep track of how much time has passed in our animation and how long the animation should be. In this case, we've chosen 300 milliseconds, as generally, somewhere between 200 and 300 milliseconds gives a decent user experience.

```
private final static long animationTime = 300;
private long animationStart = 0;
```

The animation logic all occurs within sublayout. We'll only run the animation code if verticalOffset is greater than zero, that is, only if the screen is not all the way onto the display.

If verticalOffset is greater than zero, we'll check the current time against the animationStart time. Based on the ratio of the elapsed time to the total time for the animation, we'll set a new value for verticalOffset.

Finally, after updating the screen's position, we'll queue another update layout if verticalOffset is still not zero by calling UiApplication.invokeLater.

Animating the Layout

The code for sublayout follows:

```
protected void sublayout(int width, int height) {
    super.sublayout(width, height);
    if (verticalOffset > 0) {
        if (animationStart == 0) {
            // start the animation
            animationStart = System.currentTimeMillis();
        }
        else {
            long timeElapsed = System.currentTimeMillis() - animationStart;
            if (timeElapsed >= animationTime) {
                verticalOffset = 0;
            }
            else {
                float percentDone = (float)timeElapsed / (float)animationTime;
                verticalOffset =
                    Display.getHeight() - (int)(percentDone * Display.getHeight());
            }
        }
    }
    setPosition(0, verticalOffset);

    if (verticalOffset > 0) {
        UiApplication.getUiApplication().invokeLater(new Runnable() {
            public void run() {
                updateLayout();
            }
        });
    }
}
```

Notice that there's an initial case where animationStart is zero. This case represents the first frame of the animation, so we just leave verticalOffset where it is.

Speaking of verticalOffset, we'll initialize it in the LoginScreen constructor to the height of the display:

```
verticalOffset = Display.getHeight();

new Thread(this).start();
```

And that's it. Now, the login success screen will smoothly scroll up from the bottom of the screen (see Figure 5-31).

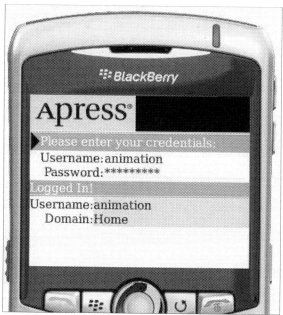

Figure 5-31. *The login success screen sliding in*

All animation follows the same basic pattern, but it can get much more complex. With the same basic technique you can implement motion, fading, and more.

Summary

Congratulations! This chapter covered a lot of ground, and by working through it, you've learned enough about the BlackBerry UI to create all kinds of great-looking applications.

In this chapter, we modified our UiFun application from last chapter by creating a new label field that allowed us to display an image alongside the label and providing a different background and foreground color. We also created a replacement button field that let us specify colors for both focused and unfocused states and gave us a slightly different look than the default ButtonField. Then, we created a new layout manager that let us align our labels and edit fields in the way we wanted and a new dialog to replace the default BlackBerry OK dialog. After that, we made some tweaks to the application's color and alignment and, finally, added a simple animation effect to the login success screen.

Individually, all these changes were small, but together, they represent the starting point for creating most of the great user interfaces you see on modern BlackBerry applications.

Now, we've gone pretty much as far as we will with the BlackBerry user interface in this book. In the next chapter, we'll start looking at an entirely new topic that'll help you produce much more capable applications—storing data on the device.

Chapter 6

Storing Data

You now know enough about the BlackBerry user interface to create some pretty impressive looking applications. So far, however, we've mostly focused on the basics of application lifecycle and user interface. The applications that we've created haven't saved any data to any form of persistent storage; each time they're run, it's as if they're running for the first time.

In the real world, most applications need to persist data. Even the simplest of applications typically has a user option or two that need to be stored when the application is shut down or the device is reset.

A number of different mechanisms exist on the BlackBerry for persisting data. Some applications use more than one method depending on what is persisted, whereas other applications choose one or another and use that. We'll list and describe the different persistence methods, explain times when you might want to use each one, and then build a couple of applications to explore the more common and useful methods in depth.

Storing Data on the BlackBerry

The BlackBerry, like most smartphones, uses flash memory to store persistent data between application and device resets. BlackBerry devices have internal flash memory, and most models also support external SD cards. Some types of persistence work with the internal memory only, while some work with both internal flash memory and any SD card that's attached to the device.

Choices for Persistence

The BlackBerry offers several ways to store persistent data on the device. In versions of the JDE prior to version 5.0, these are:

- MIDP's Record Management System (RMS)
- BlackBerry Persistent Store
- JSR 75 FileConnection support
- JDE Version 5.0 adds one more: SQLite.

Because this book is designed to help you develop for the widest range of BlackBerry devices, we'll only briefly touch on SQLite, which is only available on devices with OS 5.0 or later.

RMS

RMS is supported by BlackBerry mostly as part of supporting the MIDP standard. It's a simple, non-relational database format that enables the application to store arrays of bytes. There's minimal support for sharing data between applications, and application data is attached to the application—that is, when the application is removed from the device, application data is also removed. Generally, there's no reason to use RMS unless you're supporting legacy code or developing a MIDlet instead of a BlackBerry CLDC application, which, as we discussed in Chapter 3, is not usually an ideal choice for BlackBerry development. You can find information about RMS in many places on the Web, and in the BlackBerry Javadocs. All the relevant classes are located in the `javax.microedition.rms` package. RMS stores can be written only to the internal flash memory of the device.

Persistent Store

The BlackBerry Persistent Store provides similar features to RMS; however, it offers an easier way to store a wider range of objects and the capability to directly store instances of classes that you define in your applications. It also optionally offers compression and security with little extra work from the application, so it is the method you should use for most of your data storage functionality in a majority of BlackBerry applications. The Persistent Store classes are located in `net.rim.device.api.system`: `PersistentStore` and `PersistentObject` (`PersistentContent` provides compression and encryption). Finally, persistent stores can be written only to the device's internal flash memory.

Runtime Store

The Runtime Store is similar to the Persistent Store, but doesn't persist across device resets. It's mostly useful as a mechanism for applications to share information.

JSR 75 FileConnection

The FileConnection APIs are part of Java Specification Request (JSR) 75. JSR is part of the Java Community Process. The other part of JSR 75 includes Personal Information Management (PIM) APIs, which are also supported by the BlackBerry, but they are outside the scope of this chapter.

The FileConnection APIs allow you to access the BlackBerry file system—both the device's internal memory and any SD card that is currently plugged into the device. The file system is where the BlackBerry stores pictures, media, files that are downloaded through the browser, and any attachments saved from email, and it is generally accessible by all BlackBerry applications on the device. It's a good place to store large files, such as pictures or documents, especially if the user might want to access them in some other way, such as through the BlackBerry Desktop Manager.

SQLite

SQLite is a full SQL database implementation. It's powerful and useful for storing structured data, but because it's available only for devices that run BlackBerry OS 5.0 or later, you should use it only if you need it and are willing to target a smaller segment of BlackBerry devices.

The BlackBerry SQLite implementation enables you to create and access databases stored on the device's internal memory and external SD cards.

Your choices for persistence cover a wide enough range of functionality to meet almost any application's need. Because the Persistent Store and the FileConnection APIs are the most commonly used and cover the persistence needs of almost all applications, we'll focus on those throughout the remainder of this chapter. We'll also build a couple of applications to explore how the APIs function.

BlackBerry Persistent Store

The Persistent Store enables you to save objects to the device's flash memory. Because it doesn't support saving to the SD card, it's not a good idea to use it to store documents or anything else that can run up to large amounts of storage space. Most modern devices have at least 128 MB of flash memory onboard and typically, a significant percentage of that is free even after taking into account space used by the OS, email, and other data. This means you don't have to knock yourself out trying to save space while writing typical application data like user settings; however, if you need to manage many high-resolution photos, audio, or video files, the FileConnection API is probably a better choice, and is covered later in this chapter.

There are only two classes you really need to be familiar with to use the Persistent Store: `net.rim.device.api.system.PersistentStore` and `net.rim.device.aip.system.PersistentObject`.

Persistent Store Keys

Persistent Store manages a list of keys (long values) and objects (instances of `PersistentObject`). The list of keys is global across all applications on the device. Unfortunately, you don't know ahead of time which keys are in use by other applications; but, in practice, the keyspace is so large that conflicts never occur.

Fortunately, BlackBerry JDE and JDE Plug-in for Eclipse both offer a convenient shortcut for generating a `long` value for use as a key. Simply type some text into the editor, select it, and right-click. A menu item called *Convert String to Long* (for the Eclipse plug-in—see Figure 6-1) or *Convert [Selected Text] to long* (for the JDE—see Figure 6-2) and a new `long` value is generated based on a hash of the selected text.

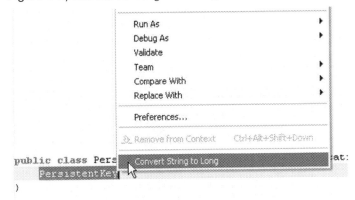

Figure 6-1. *Creating a long value for a Persistent Store key with the Eclipse plug-in*

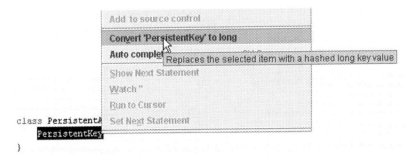

Figure 6-2. *Creating a long value for a Persistent Store key with the JDE*

Persistent Objects

Using the `PersistentStore.getPersistentObject` method returns an instance of `PersistentObject`, *even if the key hasn't ever been used before*. This is important. You always get back a `PersistentObject`, but the content of that object might be null. This means either that nothing has been saved with that key or it was deleted:

```
PersistentObject persistentObject =
PersistentStore.getPersistentObject(0x2a5c4229e4666089L);
```

The contents of the PersistentObject are accessed through the getContents method. Again, this method might return null:

```
// contents may be null
Object contents = persistentObject.getContents();
```

To set or replace the contents of the PersistentObject, use the setContents method:

```
Hashtable hashtable = new Hashtable();
persistentObject.setContents(hashtable);
```

Setting the contents, however, does not mean the object has been persisted. For that, you need to call the commit method:

```
persistentObject.commit();
```

One final note: the PersistentObject maintains a reference to its contents. To change the data in the PersistentObject,, you just need to modify that instance and call persistentObject.commit; you do not need to call setContents again, unless you want an entirely different object to be associated with the given persistent key:

```
// This will persist MyKey and New Value
// no need to call persistentObject.setContents
hashtable.put("MyKey", "New Value");
persistentObject.commit();
```

What Can You Persist?

The Persistent Store obviously can directly persist only objects, not primitive types. You can't directly persist an int, for example, but you can wrap the int in an Integer object and persist that:

```
persistentObject.setContents(new Integer(1234));
```

Generally, any object that you pass into setContents must implement the net.rim.device.api.util.Persistable interface. This interface contains no methods; it's just a marker for the BlackBerry OS. A lot of the built-in classes on the BlackBerry implement this interface. See the Javadocs for Persistable for a list.

In addition to these, a few of the basic Java classes are also allowed, even though they don't explicitly implement Persistable. These additional allowed persistable classes are:

```
java.lang.Boolean
java.lang.Byte
java.lang.Characte
java.lang.Integer
java.lang.Long
java.lang.Object
java.lang.Short
java.lang.String
java.util.Vector
java.util.Hashtable
```

Arrays of primitive types are also implicitly persistable, as are arrays of other persistable types. So, you can persist byte[], char[], int[],String[], Vector[], and so on.

Note that persistence saves the entire object, including all objects it references. This means that if your object references other objects, those objects must be persistable, too. In the previous example, we could persist the hashtable after we added a new key-value pair because the key and value were both strings, and String is persistable. However, the following would not be allowed:

```
public class MyClass {
    int someValue;
}
...

        hashtable.put("AnotherKey", new MyClass());
        // The next line will throw an exception
        // because MyClass isn't Persistable
        persistentObject.commit();
```

But if MyClass implements Persistable, everything will work:

```
public class MyClass implements Persistable {
    int someValue;
}
...

        hashtable.put("AnotherKey", new MyClass());
        // This will work now
        persistentObject.commit();
```

That's enough of the theory to get us started. We'll touch on a couple of other details later, but for now let's put this knowledge to work.

The Persistable Application

Create a new BlackBerry application project called Persistable. The main screen will have a few controls on it, so we can demonstrate persistence of different data types. To save time, here's the code for both classes:

PersistenceApplication.java

```
package com.beginningblackberry.persistence;

import net.rim.device.api.ui.UiApplication;

public class PersistenceApplication extends UiApplication {
    public PersistenceApplication() {
        PersistenceScreen screen = new PersistenceScreen();
        pushScreen(screen);
    }

    public static void main(String[] args) {
        PersistenceApplication application = new PersistenceApplication();
        application.enterEventDispatcher();
    }

}
```

PersistenceScreen.java

```
package com.beginningblackberry.persistence;
```

```
import java.io.IOException;
import java.util.Hashtable;

import net.rim.device.api.system.PersistentObject;
import net.rim.device.api.system.PersistentStore;
import net.rim.device.api.ui.component.CheckboxField;
import net.rim.device.api.ui.component.DateField;
import net.rim.device.api.ui.component.EditField;
import net.rim.device.api.ui.component.NumericChoiceField;
import net.rim.device.api.ui.container.MainScreen;
public class PersistenceScreen extends MainScreen {
    EditField editField;

    public PersistenceScreen() {
        editField = new EditField("Persistent Data:", "");
        add(editField);
    }

}
```

We intentionally kept this simple. The application will save data when you exit and load that data into the appropriate UI components when you start the application.

Note that we added a bunch of imports to `PersistenceScreen` here to save time later on.

The Persistent Object

We need to have the persistent object available to load and save data. We'll make it an instance variable of `PersistenceScreen`:

```
public class PersistenceScreen extends MainScreen {
    PersistentObject persistentObject;
```

Now let's define the key. Right under the `PersistentObject` declaration, type "com.thinkingblackberry.persistence.PersistenceScreen," and then highlight it and select Convert String to Long:

```
public class PersistenceScreen extends MainScreen {
    PersistentObject persistentObject;
    0x9df9f961bc6d6baL
```

You should get the same long value as above if you started with the same string (don't worry if you didn't; it's not important for this exercise. As long as you have some value, the application will still work).

Finally, add the following to make it a static final long variable:

```
public class PersistenceScreen extends MainScreen {
    PersistentObject persistentObject;
    static final long KEY = 0x9df9f961bc6d6baL;
```

Now add the following line to the constructor to initialize the object:

```
                persistentObject = PersistentStore.getPersistentObject(KEY);
```

Loading the Data

Loading is easy in this case. We'll store a string directly into the contents of the PersistentObject so we'll check to see whether a string was set, and if so, update the edit field:

```
if (persistentObject.getContents() != null) {

editField.setText((String)persistentObject.getContents());
    }
```

The Save Method

We'll start by saving the data. This introduces another new UI concept; the screen's save method. Every screen on the BlackBerry keeps track of whether its controls have been modified since it was displayed. If they have, it displays a Save/Discard/Cancel prompt to the user. If the user chooses "Save," the save method is called. By overriding that method, you can save your data when the screen is closed.

Add the following code to PersistenceScreen:

```
public void save() throws IOException {
        persistentObject.setContents(editField.getText());
        persistentObject.commit();
    }
```

That's all you have to do! Now go ahead and run the application. The first time, you'll see the edit field is empty, as shown in Figure 6-3.

Figure 6-3. *Persistence application before entering any data*

Now enter some text into the edit field and click the Escape key to exit the application. The Save prompt displays as shown in Figure 6-4.

Figure 6-4. *The Save prompt*

Select Save, and the application exits. Now when you restart the application, the text displays in the edit field just as you entered it (see Figure 6-5).

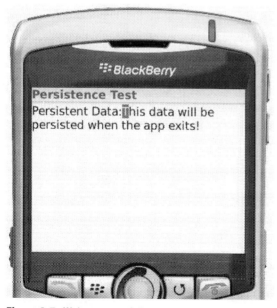

Figure 6-5. *We've successfully saved and loaded data!*

More Advanced Persistence

The initial example was just to give you an idea of how easy persistence can be. We'll now modify the application to do something that might be a little more applicable in a real-world application.

The Persistent Store's use of long values for keys, and the method of wrapping each stored object in a PersistentObject makes it easy to store individual objects, but what if (as in most applications) you need to store a lot of different pieces of data? You can use a different long key for each one, but that rapidly gets unmanageable. The solution is to store a java.util.Hashtable in the PersistentObject, and then store each piece of data within that hashtable. A Hashtable stores a set of key-value pairs, and as long as all the keys and all the values are persistable objects, you can persist the hashtable itself.

Modifying the UI

To give us some more data to store, we'll add a few fields to the PersistenceScreen. Add the following to the top of the PersistenceScreen class:

```
CheckboxField checkboxField;
NumericChoiceField numericChoiceField;
DateField dateField;
```

And the following lines to the constructor:

```
checkboxField = new CheckboxField("Boolean data", false);
numericChoiceField = new NumericChoiceField("Numeric data:",
1, 10, 1);
dateField = new DateField("Date:",
System.currentTimeMillis(), DateField.DATE);

add(checkboxField);
add(numericChoiceField);
add(dateField);
```

NumericChoiceField basically acts the same as the ObjectChoiceField you saw earlier, but contains only integer values and has a couple of methods to make getting and setting the values as ints easy. DateField naturally enough displays a date and time as represented in Java as a long value.

Using a Hashtable

We're going to make the persistent object use a Hashtable to store its contents, instead of storing a String. Add a declaration for the Hashtable to the top of PersistenceScreen:

```
public class PersistenceScreen extends MainScreen {
    Hashtable persistentHashtable;
```

The idea in the constructor is to create the Hashtable if this is the first time using the Persistent Store, or load it if not. Change the initialization code for the PersistentObject to the following:

```
    if (persistentObject.getContents() == null) {
        persistentHashtable = new Hashtable();
        persistentObject.setContents(persistentHashtable);
    }
    else {
        persistentHashtable = (Hashtable)persistentObject.getContents();
    }
```

Loading and Saving the Data

With the hashtable initialized, add the following lines to the end of the
PersistenceScreen constructor to load the data:

```
    if (persistentHashtable.containsKey("EditData")) {
        editField.setText((String)persistentHashtable.get("EditData"));
    }
    if (persistentHashtable.containsKey("BoolData")) {
        Boolean booleanObject = (Boolean)persistentHashtable.get("BoolData");
        checkboxField.setChecked(booleanObject.booleanValue());
    }
    if (persistentHashtable.containsKey("IntData")) {
        Integer intObject = (Integer)persistentHashtable.get("IntData");
        numericChoiceField.setSelectedValue(intObject.intValue());
    }
    if (persistentHashtable.containsKey("Date")) {
        Long longObject = (Long)persistentHashtable.get("Date");
        dateField.setDate(longObject.longValue());
    }
```

The pattern is the same for all primitive datatypes. Wrap them in the appropriate
associated data class and put that into the hashtable.

The save method is simpler because we don't have to do all the checking:

```
    public void save() throws IOException {
        persistentHashtable.put("EditData", editField.getText());
        persistentHashtable.put("BoolData", new Boolean(checkboxField.getChecked()));
        persistentHashtable.put("IntData", new
Integer(numericChoiceField.getSelectedValue()));
        persistentHashtable.put("Date", new Long(dateField.getDate()));
        persistentObject.commit();
    }
```

Notice we removed the setContents method from save. The PersistentObject
maintains a reference to the Hashtable throughout the lifecycle of the screen, so all we
need to do is call commit and it will write the latest versions of all referenced data to
persistent storage.

Clearing the Old Persistent Data from the Simulator

There's one last thing we need to do before running the application. Because we're using the same Persistent Store key as before, and because we've already persisted a `String` using that key, the first time we try to read the contents of the `PersistentObject` and cast to a `Hashtable`, we'll get an exception because the contents are a `String`. We need to clear the simulator's persistent data before running the application again.

From the JDE Plug-in for Eclipse, you erase the simulator's file system by selecting the BlackBerry menu, Erase Simulator File ➤ Erase File System (see Figure 6-6).

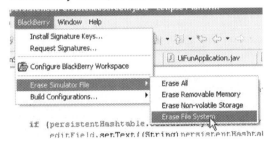

Figure 6-6. *You need to erase the file system to erase the old contents of the Persistent Store.*

From the JDE, the same functionality is available from the File menu, Erase Simulator File, Erase File System.

You might wonder about how we'd deal with this situation on a real device. This does happen, and we'll touch on that in shortly, but right now, let's look at the new application in action (see Figure 6-7). The usage is the same, but now we're storing a bunch of different pieces of data:

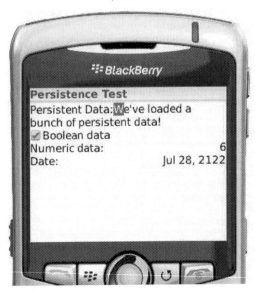

Figure 6-7. *Storing and loading a bunch of data*

Clearing Persistent Data from a Device

On a BlackBerry device, persistent data is somewhat independent of the application. What does that mean? It has to do with what types of classes you persist. If you persist only classes that are defined in the BlackBerry API, your data by default will stay behind when your application is deleted from the device. Other applications can still access it, and if you reload your application onto the device, your data will still be there.

If you want your data to be removed when your application is removed, the easiest method is to store classes that are defined in your application. In our application, this is easy to accomplish. We'll define a new class called CustomHashtable that extends Hashtable. Remember, we have to be sure to make it implement Persistable because any class that we want to persist must *directly* implement Persistable; it doesn't matter if it extends a persistable class. Create the class in a new file called CustomHashtable.java, containing the following code:

```
package com.beginningblackberry.persistence;

import java.util.Hashtable;

import net.rim.device.api.util.Persistable;

public class CustomHashtable extends Hashtable implements Persistable {

}
```

We don't need to add anything more to this class. Just replace all the references to Hashtable in PersistableScreen with references to CustomHashtable and everything will work as before, except that when the application is removed from the device, the data will not stay behind.

The FileConnection API

The JSR 75 FileConnection API gives your application the capability to read and write to the BlackBerry file system, both the internal flash memory and any memory card attached to your device. It also enables you to read data that other applications have written to the file system. This is especially useful for retrieving pictures, video, and other media that might be on your device.

In the following sections, we'll create a simple application to browse for photos from the device's memory (internal or memory card) and display them on screen.

Basic Application Framework

You should be used to creating applications by now; create a new a new BlackBerry application called FileConnection. Start with an application class and main screen class. The initial classes are as follows:

FileConnectionApplication.java:

```java
package com.thinkingblackberry.fileconnection;

import net.rim.device.api.ui.UiApplication;

public class FileConnectionApplication extends UiApplication {

    public FileConnectionApplication() {
        FileConnectionScreen screen = new FileConnectionScreen();
        pushScreen(screen);
    }

    public static void main(String[] args) {
        FileConnectionApplication app = new FileConnectionApplication();
        app.enterEventDispatcher();
    }

}
```

FileConnectionScreen.java:

```java
package com.thinkingblackberry.fileconnection;

import net.rim.device.api.ui.MenuItem;
import net.rim.device.api.ui.component.Menu;
import net.rim.device.api.ui.component.ObjectListField;
import net.rim.device.api.ui.container.MainScreen;

public class FileConnectionScreen extends MainScreen {
    private ObjectListField fileList;
    private String currentPath = "file:///";

    public FileConnectionScreen() {
        setTitle("FileConnection");

        fileList = new ObjectListField();
        fileList.set(new String[] {"store/", "SDCard/"});

        add(fileList);
    }

    protected void makeMenu(Menu menu, int instance) {
        super.makeMenu(menu, instance);
        menu.add(new MenuItem("Select", 10, 10) {
            public void run() {
                loadFile();
            }
        });
    }

    private void loadFile()  {
    }

}
```

We're introducing another new UI component here: the ObjectListField. This displays a vertical list of strings on screen. We'll use it to show the contents of the directories as we browse.

We've populated our object list field with two initial entries: store/ and SDCard/. These are the root directories for the internal device memory and the memory card, respectively, and are the same on every BlackBerry device. We use them as a starting point for browsing.

There's also a String that contains the current path. When opening a FileConnection, you need the full path. we'll use this variable to keep track of it.

Finally, we've added a single menu item in the makeMenu method using an anonymous inner class as discussed in Chapter 4. We've also created a loadFile method that will contain all the FileConnection logic.

For now, the application looks like Figure 6-8, with the default two items in the ObjectListField and the single custom menu item.

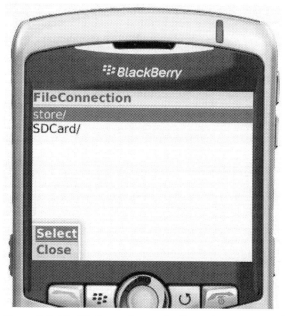

Figure 6-8. *The FileConnection application main screen containing the two default directory entries*

Opening a File Connection

Classes related to the FileConnection API are found in the javax.microedition.io.file package. For this application, we'll mostly work with the FileConnection interface.

FileConnection is a pretty rich interface. It enables you to create and delete files, list the contents of a directory, and read and write file contents and attributes.

You obtain a FileConnection using the javax.microedition.io.Connector class. The Connector class is also used to initiate network connections among other things, so we'll be using it again in the future. All of its methods take a string parameter, which is a URL representing a resource. Connector URLs conform to the standard URL definition from RFC 2396, with a scheme portion (such as http:) that represents the type of resource being requested.

The BlackBerry Javadocs thoroughly explain the details of the many different connection types; we'll explore some of them in Chapter 7 when we discuss networking. For now, just be concerned with opening file resources.

File connection URLs start with "file://."

For example, to open the store directory representing the device's internal memory, you'd use the following code. Note the extra "/" at the beginning of the URL:

```
try {
    FileConnection storeDirectory =
(FileConnection)Connector.open("file:///store/");
    } catch (IOException e) {
    }
```

As long as the URL represents a path that *could* be valid, no exception is thrown. This enables you to create a file by first opening a connection to a URL representing the file you want to create, and then calling FileConnection.create. For BlackBerry, a URL is valid if all directories specified in the URL exist, with the exception of the last one only if the path returns a file. For example, if the home directory exists under the store directory, and is empty (containing no subdirectories or files) then the following URL is allowed:

```
file://store/home/testfile.txt
```

and so is the following:

```
file://store/home/newdir/
```

but the following URL will cause an exception to be thrown, because newdir doesn't exist:

```
file://store/home/newdir/test.txt
```

Listing the Directory Contents

The first thing we'll implement is listing files and subdirectories in a directory. Whenever you click the Select menu item, if the currently highlighted item in the object list field is a directory, we'll replace the items in the list field with the contents of that directory.

When the user clicks Select, we'll construct a path to that directory by simply concatenating the current path with the path of that directory; all directory entries end with a "/"character so we don't have to worry about adding that.

The FileConnection.isDirectory method tells you if the file connection points to a directory. If it does, the list method retrieves an Enumeration of Strings, which are the pathnames of the files and directories contained within the directory. Because ObjectListField requires an Object array, we'll add the strings from the enumeration one by one to a Vector, and get the array from that Vector when we're done. Here's the code for loadFile:

```
private void loadFile() {
    currentPath += fileList.get(fileList, fileList.getSelectedIndex());
    try {
        FileConnection fileConnection = (FileConnection)Connector.open(currentPath);
        if (fileConnection.isDirectory()) {
            Enumeration directoryEnumerator = fileConnection.list();
            Vector contentVector = new Vector();
            while(directoryEnumerator.hasMoreElements()) {

                contentVector.addElement(directoryEnumerator.nextElement());
            }
            String[] directoryContents = new String[contentVector.size()];
            contentVector.copyInto(directoryContents);
            fileList.set(directoryContents);
        }

    } catch (IOException ex) {

    }
}
```

Run the application, and you should be able to navigate through the device's file system by selecting directories and clicking the Select menu item (see Figure 6-9).

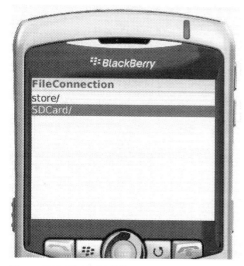

Figure 6-9. *Highlight SDCard, and then open the menu and click Select.*

Highlight BlackBerry, and then open the menu and click Select.

Browsing through the SD card's file structure

Viewing Pictures

Now we'll add the code to loadFile to actually view pictures. We will create a new screen containing a single BitmapField to view our picture; whenever we highlight a picture in the file list and click Select, we'll create a new instance of this screen and push it onto the stack.

The Image Display Screen

Make a new file called ImageDisplayScreen.java in your project. The code for ImageDisplayScreen is simple:

```java
package com.thinkingblackberry.fileconnection;

import net.rim.device.api.system.EncodedImage;
import net.rim.device.api.ui.component.BitmapField;
import net.rim.device.api.ui.container.MainScreen;

public class ImageDisplayScreen extends MainScreen {
    public ImageDisplayScreen(EncodedImage image) {
        BitmapField bitmapField = new BitmapField();
        bitmapField.setImage(image);
        add(bitmapField);
    }
}
```

This uses an EncodedImage instead of a Bitmap because that's the way we'll load the image from the file system. EncodedImage has a few extra features over Bitmap including scaling, support for multiple frames, and support for more file types.

Loading Images from the File System

For any FileConnection, you can retrieve an InputStream. This enables us to read bytes from the file.

The only checking that we're doing is that the path ends in a known file extension. For purposes of this exercise, you don't need to worry about error handling, but if this were a production application, we'd add more. The following code should be added to loadFile, right after the if statement:

```
else if (currentPath.endsWith(".jpg") || currentPath.endsWith(".png")) {
    InputStream inputStream = fileConnection.openInputStream();
    InputStream inputStream = fileConnection.openInputStream();
    byte[] imageBytes = new byte[(int)fileConnection.fileSize()];
    inputStream.read(imageBytes);
    inputStream.close();
    EncodedImage eimg = EncodedImage.createEncodedImage(imageBytes, 0,
imageBytes.length);

    UiApplication.getUiApplication().pushScreen(new ImageDisplayScreen(eimg));


}
```

Getting Images into the Simulator

Before you run the application, you need a few pictures on the simulator's file system to use for testing. You can get these by running the camera application on your simulator. If you have a webcam attached to or built in to your PC, you might get to snap an actual picture. Otherwise, you are presented with a dialog box to choose an image to represent the picture the camera takes. In either case, take a picture or two and start the FileConnection application again.

Unless you explicitly saved your picture to a different location, navigate to SDCard/BlackBerry/pictures, and you should see the image listed, as shown in Figure 6-10.

Figure 6-10. *A list of images in the pictures directory*

If you click on one of those images, you should see something like Figure 6-11.

Figure 6-11. *The image?*

You might get a clearer image if you selected a lower resolution picture from the dialog box, but if you took a higher-resolution picture using the camera on a real device, what you see is the extreme upper left corner of that photo.

The BlackBerry's LCD screen is generally a lot lower resolution than its camera, so to display the full image, you need to scale it. This is another reason we used EncodedImage instead of Bitmap; it has better built-in image-scaling support.

Scaling the Image

Though not directly relevant to persistent storage, scaling the image will make the application complete, and it is useful to know how to do it

We'll do the image scaling within ImageDisplayScreen's constructor. We'll present the code first and discuss it after. The new constructor for ImageDisplayScreen is:

```
public ImageDisplayScreen(EncodedImage image) {
    int displayWidth = Fixed32.toFP(Display.getWidth());
    int imageWidth = Fixed32.toFP(image.getWidth());
    int scalingFactor = Fixed32.div(imageWidth, displayWidth);
    EncodedImage scaledImage = image.scaleImage32(scalingFactor, scalingFactor);
    BitmapField bitmapField = new BitmapField();
    bitmapField.setImage(scaledImage);
    add(bitmapField);
}
```

> **NOTE:** EncodedImage uses 32-bit fixed point decimal numbers as its scale factors. The BlackBerry provides support for numbers in this format in the net.rim.device. api.math.Fixed32 class. Fixed32 enables you to store a decimal number in a 32-bit int; 16 bits are used for the integer portion and 16 bits are used for the decimal portion. Addition and subtraction operations on Fixed32 numbers are faster than on floats or doubles, so they can be a good choice for those types of decimal arithmetic. When using Fixed32 numbers, remember to convert back and forth from regular ints; that's what the toFP method does. You also must use Fixed32 methods for multiplying and dividing Fixed32 format numbers. Using the * and / operators produces nonsensical results, but you can use the standard Java + and − operators for addition and subtraction.

For EncodedImage, a scaling factor of between 0 and 1 means scale up; a scaling factor of greater than 1 means scale down. We can get the correct scaling factor for our image by dividing the image's width by the BlackBerry display's width. To be completely precise, we could check the image and display height, too, but I'll leave that as an exercise for you. When you run the FileConnection application and select the same image now, you'll get a much better picture (see Figure 6-12).

Figure 6-12. *The correctly scaled image*

This is as far as we'll go with reading files from the file system. There are, of course, areas where the application can be improved, but at this point, you should have a good understanding of how to read files and directories using the FileConnection API. You can also try to run this application on a real device, and you should be able to view photos that were taken by the device's camera.

Now let's explore the other half of the FileConnection API: creating and writing to files on the file system.

Writing to the File System

We'll extend the FileConnection application to enable writing to the file system. We can leverage the same directory browsing code and add functionality that enables you to make a copy of an existing image in the same directory.

The functionality will be as follows: when a file (not a directory) is highlighted, a Copy menu item is available. When you click this menu item, you are prompted for a name for the new file, and if that file name doesn't exist, the selected file is copied into a new file with the specified name.

A Dynamic Menu Item

First, we'll add the new menu item to let us copy the currently selected file. Before we add the menu item, let's put in place the method that we'll call to do the work of copying the file. Add this to FileConnectionScreen:

```
        private void copyFile() {
}
```

Now we want the Copy menu item to show up only when a file is selected. We know which entries in the object list field are files because the directories all end with the "/"character. Because we're constructing the menu in the makeMenu method, which is called every time the menu key is clicked, we can easily check at that time if the currently selected item ends in "/"", and add the Copy menu item only if it does not. Add the following code to the FileConnectionScreen's makeMenu method:

```
        String selectedItem = (String)fileList.get(fileList,
fileList.getSelectedIndex());
        if (!selectedItem.endsWith("/")) {
            menu.add(new MenuItem("Copy", 10, 10) {
                public void run() {
                    copyFile();
                }
            });
        }
```

If you run the application now and browse around, you'll see that the Copy menu item shows up only when a file is highlighted (see Figure 6-13).

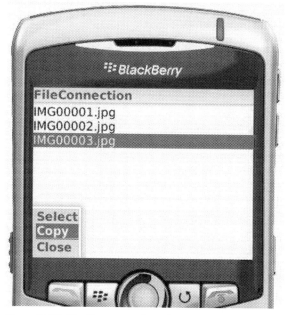

Figure 6-13. *The Copy menu item shows up only when a file is selected.*

The File Name Screen

When we copy a file, we'll pop up a dialog asking for a name for the new copy. This requires us to create a new screen with an edit field for the name. We'll subclass net.rim.device.api.container.PopupScreen to get a dialog rather than a full screen. Note that the constructor for PopupScreen asks for the delegate manager, just as the constructor for Screen does. We'll just use a VerticalFieldManager. We'll also add a ButtonField so there's some way to dismiss the screen (remember to set the ButtonField.CONSUME_CLICK style).

Finally, we'll provide a method in the screen class to retrieve the name of the file from the edit field. The FileNameScreen class looks like this:

```
package com.thinkingblackberry.fileconnection;

import net.rim.device.api.ui.Field;
import net.rim.device.api.ui.FieldChangeListener;
import net.rim.device.api.ui.component.ButtonField;
import net.rim.device.api.ui.component.EditField;
import net.rim.device.api.ui.container.PopupScreen;
import net.rim.device.api.ui.container.VerticalFieldManager;

public class FileNameScreen extends PopupScreen implements FieldChangeListener {
    private EditField fileNameField;
    private ButtonField okButton;
    public FileNameScreen() {
        super(new VerticalFieldManager());

        fileNameField = new EditField("New Filename:", "");
        add(fileNameField);
        okButton = new ButtonField("OK", ButtonField.CONSUME_CLICK |
Field.FIELD_HCENTER);
        okButton.setChangeListener(this);
        add(okButton);
    }

    public String getFilename() {
        return fileNameField.getText();
    }

    public void fieldChanged(Field field, int context) {
        if (field == okButton) {
            close();
        }
    }
}
```

Copying the File

To display the file name screen, we'll use UiApplication.pushModalScreen instead of pushScreen. This just means that the method won't return until the file name screen is closed, this is the functionality we want in this case because we can't copy the file until you've entered a file name and clicked OK:

```
FileNameScreen screen = new FileNameScreen();
UiApplication.getUiApplication().pushModalScreen(screen);
String newFilename = screen.getFilename();
```

After getting the file name, we'll open a connection to the full URL for that filename and use FileConnection.exists to check to see if there's already a file there. If so, we'll display a dialog and exit the method:

```
FileConnection newFileConnection =
(FileConnection)Connector.open(currentPath + newFilename);
    if (newFileConnection.exists()) {
        Dialog.alert("The file '" + newFilename + "' already exists!");
        newFileConnection.close();
        return;
    }
```

If the file doesn't exist, call FileConnection.create to create it. Then, open an OutputStream to the new file:

```
                            newFileConnection.create();
                            OutputStream newFileOutputStream =
newFileConnection.openOutputStream();
```

From that point on, the code is the same as when loading an image, except that instead of constructing an image with the byte array, we're writing it to the OutputStream that represents the newly created file. Here's copyFile in its entirety:

```
private void copyFile() {
    // Prompt for the new filename
    FileNameScreen screen = new FileNameScreen();
    UiApplication.getUiApplication().pushModalScreen(screen);
    String newFilename = screen.getFilename();

    try {
        FileConnection newFileConnection =
(FileConnection)Connector.open(currentPath + newFilename);
        if (newFileConnection.exists()) {
            Dialog.alert("The file '" + newFilename + "' already exists!");
            newFileConnection.close();
            return;
        }

        // The file doesn't exist, so we'll create it
        newFileConnection.create();
        OutputStream newFileOutputStream = newFileConnection.openOutputStream();

        // Open the old file
        currentPath += fileList.get(fileList, fileList.getSelectedIndex());
```

```
FileConnection fileConnection = (FileConnection)Connector.open(currentPath);
InputStream inputStream = fileConnection.openInputStream();


// Copy the contents of the old file into the new one
byte[] fileContents = new byte[(int)fileConnection.fileSize()];
inputStream.read(fileContents);
newFileOutputStream.write(fileContents, 0, fileContents.length);
inputStream.close();
newFileOutputStream.close();
Dialog.inform("Successfully copied the file!");
} catch (IOException ex) {

}
}
```

Now run the application to try it out. Browse to the SDCard/BlackBerry/pictures folder and copy one of the files there. Figure 6-14 shows the Filename dialog.

Figure 6-14. *Entering the new file name; be sure to include the correct extension.*

because our application doesn't dynamically reload the directory, you have to exit and browse back to the pictures directory to see your new file (see Figure 6-15).

Figure 6-15. *The new file*

You can select and view this file just as you could the original.

Summary

You should now have a good understanding of how to use persistence on the BlackBerry; at least you've experienced a couple of the most used and most useful methods. We built an application that saved and loaded a few different types of data using the BlackBerry Persistent Store, and we created and saved our own persistent class. We also created an application that used the FileConnection API to browse through the BlackBerry file system and view an image stored in it, and then we extended the application to enable us to write a copy of that image back to the file system. Using these mechanisms, your potential universe of BlackBerry applications has suddenly expanded. You can now create applications that save data between invocations, and there are many commercial applications that don't require any more knowledge of BlackBerry programming than you've already developed.

Congratulate yourself for getting this far, and get ready. We're about to expand the reach of your BlackBerry applications even further—literally—because in the next chapter, you learn how to create applications that can send and receive data over a wireless network.

Chapter 7

Hello Out There! Making a Network-Enabled Application

The BlackBerry was built to communicate. Sending and receiving email, browsing the Web, and often even downloading applications to your device require access to the wireless data network. Naturally, a lot of the most compelling BlackBerry applications also heavily feature networking as a core part of their functionalities.

Fortunately, the BlackBerry JDE makes networking a snap. It offers a range of choices for getting your application to communicate with servers and other systems on the Internet or on a corporate network. For the most part, you don't have to worry about different device or wireless network characteristics; the BlackBerry platform abstracts that detail so you can concentrate on application-specific details.

In this chapter, we'll discuss the BlackBerry data networking functionality, the different methods that a BlackBerry can use to connect, and when and how you might want to use them. We'll then develop a couple of applications to explore making HTTP and TCP socket connections to interact with a web application on the internet.

Different Ways to Connect

The BlackBerry offers a number of different methods of making network connections. These include the BlackBerry Enterprise Server / BlackBerry Mobile Data System (BES/MDS), direct Transmission Control Procotol / Internet Protocol (TCP/IP), BlackBerry Internet Service (BIS), WiFi, Wireless Access Protocol (WAP) 1.0, and WAP 2.0. (See Figure 7-1.) They each have certain advantages and disadvantages, and depending on the configuration of your device and environment, some of the methods might not be available. Generally, you can make all supported types of network connections: HTTP connections and TCP and UDP sockets over any of these connection methods. We'll briefly cover the different connection methods.

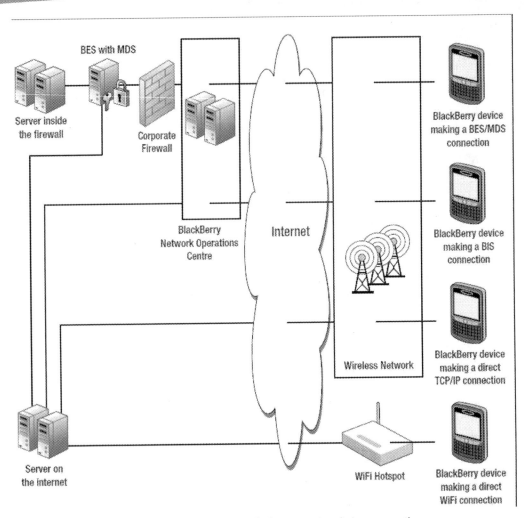

Figure 7-1. *Some of the different ways a BlackBerry device can make wireless connections*

BES/MDS

The BES allows BlackBerry devices to make network connections securely to servers inside a corporate network. This is accomplished through the MDS component of the BES, so connections made this way are sometimes referred to as BES/MDS connections. Connections made by the BlackBerry device using the MDS are actually proxied by the MDS; that is, the MDS makes connections on behalf of the BlackBerry device, and data is transferred to and from the device over the same secure channel that corporate BlackBerry email uses.

Obviously, the BES/MDS connection method is available only to devices that have been activated on a BES. The advantage to using the BES/MDS is that because the MDS makes connections, it can resolve any servers that can be reached from the server running the BES, meaning the servers behind the corporate firewall are reachable. The disadvantage is that if there are any restrictions on connections going from the BES to servers outside the network, those restrictions affect BlackBerry connections made through the BES, too.

Note that by default, the browser on devices attached to a BES uses the MDS to make connections, meaning you can use the browser to access internal web servers. In fact, this is a good way to tell if your device uses the MDS to make connections; if the title of your browser application is called "BlackBerry Browser," then your device uses the MDS tomake connections.

Direct TCP/IP

Just like most other smart phones, BlackBerry devices can also make direct TCP/IP connections using the wireless carrier's infrastructure without going through any BlackBerry-specific service. This method works with most devices, although it can be disabled by a BES administrator for devices connected to a BES.

The advantages are that this method is available on almost all BlackBerry devices. Occasionally, configuration problems with the Access Point Name (APN) used in direct TCP/IP connections (see the note) that can cause problems with TCP/IP connections. Also, though it's becoming rarer, some BlackBerry wireless plans don't include direct TCP/IP access.

NOTE: The BlackBerry device uses the)APN to make direct TCP/IP connections. The APN varies from carrier to carrier, and usually it is preconfigured on the device by the carrier; however, in some cases the configuration might have been lost. You can access APN configuration from the device Options by selecting Advanced Options ➤ TCP/IP. Some carriers require a username and password along with the APN. A search on the internet will usually provide a list of settings for the major wireless carriers.

You can also specify the APN, username, and password if necessary when making your connection. This is tricky to manage with so many configurations and is outside the scope of this book; for more information, see the BlackBerry JavaDocs for `javax.microedition.io.Connector`.

BIS

BIS provides much of the same functionality for individual BlackBerry users as the BES does for corporate users, without the same level of security. If you use a BlackBerry device that's not connected to a BES, you're already using the BIS to send and receive your email. The BIS is also able to proxy connections in the same way as the BES/MDS does. Because the BIS can access servers only on the internet, it doesn't give the access to a corporate network that using the BES/MDS does. The main advantage to using a BIS connection over a direct TCP/IP connection is that some BlackBerry wireless plans don't include direct TCP/IP access, but almost all include BIS access as it's required for non-BES email. To enable your application to make connections through the BIS, you must be part of the BlackBerry Alliance Program and receive approval for your application to use the BIS. For that reason, we won't cover BIS connections in this book, but the basic mechanism is similar to the other connection types.

WiFi

Many BlackBerry devices include WiFi networking (802.11 B/G and sometimes A). This allows your device to connect to a network via a WiFi router. You generally must set up access for specific WiFi routers. This is up to the device user, not the application developer. Assuming the device has been connected to a WiFi router, however, your application can make network connections over WiFi. The advantages are better speed, lower latency, and the fact that no carrier data charges are incurred. The disadvantage is that WiFi coverage is not as widespread as wireless network coverage for most users, so you should support at least one other connection method.

In the case of applications using a BES/MDS or BIS connection, the device can be configured to automatically use an appropriate WiFi hotspot where available to connect to the BES or BIS. This requires no additional effort on the part of the application; it's handled automatically by the BlackBerry platform. You can, however, also make a direct WiFi connection explicitly from the application.

WAP 2.0

WAP 2.0 connects through the wireless carrier's WAP gateway. Similar to direct TCP/IP connections, WAP 2.0 doesn't use any BlackBerry specific infrastructure. The wireless plan associated with the BlackBerry device must also support WAP 2.0 access. Fortunately, this is the case with almost all devices sold. The big advantage of WAP 2.0 over direct TCP/IP is that no APN configuration is necessary, meaning that devices are more likely to be able to connect without needing any additional configuration.

WAP 1.0

Unlike all the other connection methods mentioned, WAP 1.0 doesn't support the full range of connection types. Specifically, security is limited. Though WAP 1.0 is supported by all BlackBerry devices, its limitations mean that unless you have a specific reason, you should use the other connection methods instead.

Recommendation

By default the BlackBerry uses the BES/MDS as the connection method for devices activated on a BES, and it uses the TCP/IP connection method for other devices. For devices activated on a BES, this is reasonable behavior because the BES connection is at least as secure as a direct TCP/IP connection. For devices not activated on a BES, a good method is to attempt to use WAP 2.0 first because a given device is more likely to be configured to use WAP 2.0 correctly and fallback to direct TCP/IP if necessary. We'll cover how to do that later in this chapter. If you're using BES/MDS, you can rely on the automatic WiFi fallback behavior. If you're using direct TCP/IP, you might want to provide some WiFi functionality, depending on how heavily your application uses the network.

Service Book

The BlackBerry service book is a configuration storage system that the device uses to maintain information about various aspects of its configuration. The service book contains records that govern everything from optional applications that are installed or visible to email account configuration. The service book records are also used to maintain information about the different connection methods available to a given device.

You can see the service book on a BlackBerry device (or the BlackBerry simulator) by opening device Options and then clicking Advanced Options and Service Book (see Figure 7-2):

Figure 7-2. *Some typical service book records on a BlackBerry device*

Each record contains two identifiers, a CID and a UID. The UID uniquely identifies the record on the device, and the CID gives information about what type of record it is. For example, on a device with more than an associated email address, there are many service records with a CID of CMIME, but each will have a different UID.

The service book is important for networked applications because most of the connection methods have an associated record, and this can be a quick way to check to see if your device has been provisioned correctly for a given connection type. The one exception is direct TCP/IP, which doesn't have an associated service record. Configuration information for direct TCP/IP connections is specified in the TCP/IP options screen as discussed previously.

There are many different types of service book records. It can be interesting to look through them and see what's available; you shouldn't try to change or delete anything unless you know what you're doing. For the purposes of this chapter, we'll explore only the specific service records that we need.

The MIDP Connection Framework

The BlackBerry uses the same connection framework as defined in the MIDP standard, with some extra functionality specific to the BlackBerry platform.

Connector

All connections are initiated using the javax.microedition.io.Connector class. We briefly used this class in Chapter 6 to open a connection to the file system. The same class is used for HTTP, HTTPS, socket, and many other connection types.

For example, to open an HTTP connection to retrieve a web page, use the following:

```
HttpConnection connection = (HttpConnection)Connector.open("http://www.apress.com/");
```

Note that this just retrieves the primary content of the page. To get images and other resources, you'd have to request them specifically.

Connections

All the Connector.open methods return a subclass of the javax.microedition.io.Connection interface.
The specific type depends on the *scheme* of the URL passed in (the http:// portion). There's a fairly hefty hierarchy of connection types, but for most purposes you'll directly use only a few, as shown in Table 7-1.

Table 7-1. **Common Network Connection Types, Connection Interface that Connector Returns, and the URL Scheme Indicating Each Type**

Connection Type	Connection Class	URL Scheme
HTTP	HttpConnection	http://
HTTPS (secure HTTP over TLS)	HttpsConnection	https://
TCP/IP socket	SocketConnection	socket://
SSL or TLS secure socket	SecureConnection	ssl:// or tls://

All of the previous network connection types allow a similar format for the URL:

scheme://host:port/path[optional parameters]

For example:

```
                    HttpConnection connection =
(HttpConnection)Connector.open("http://www.apress.com:80/book/catalog");

SocketConnection socket = SocketConnection)Connector.open("socket://www.apress.com:80");
```

We used `FileConnection` in the previous chapter, which, as you saw, uses the `file://` scheme.

HTTP Basics

Because we'll explore HTTP networking first, we've included a quick review of the basics of the protocol. If you're familiar with HTTP, you can probably safely skip this section, but we want to briefly cover the basics of how the protocol works before we continue to ensure all the terms we use are fresh in your mind.

HTTP is the fundamental protocol of the World Wide Web. It's a connectionless request-response protocol, meaning there is no concept of a persistent connection between a series of requests.

Request and Response

An HTTP *request* is a message sent from the client (in this case, the BlackBerry device) to the server. The server sends back a *response.* The request and response might contain some content called the *body*. In addition, the response always contains a numeric *response code*, which lets us know if the request was successful, if it failed, or if more action is needed. It gives more detailed information about what exactly happened (e.g. the cause of failure).

Methods

HTTP supports several request *methods*, which help the server know how to handle the request. The most important HTTP methods for our purposes are:

- `GET`: Used to retrieve a resource (such as a web page or image) from a URL

- `POST`: Used to send data to a server (such as the content of a form) based on a URL

In fact, the BlackBerry supports only the `GET`, `POST`, and `HEAD` methods; it doesn't support custom methods. For most applications, this is sufficient, but it is something to keep in mind.

Headers

Finally, in addition to the main content of the request and response (the *body*), HTTP allows additional data to be sent in the form of *headers.* They can be sent with the request to the server and the response from the server, and they can contain arbitrary text data. There are many standard headers, and the connection API contains methods for easily accessing some of the most common ones.

The Test Web Application

I created a simple web application to let you easily explore performing HTTP POSTs and GETs from the BlackBerry (See Figure 7-3). You can access this application using your browser at `http://beginningblackberry.appspot.com`:

Apress®
Go!

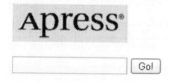

Figure 7-3. *The Test Web Application*

It consists of a single HTML page containing a PNG image and a text box. When you enter text into the box and click Go! it displays the words you typed in reverse order, one per line with an HTML line break tag between them (see Figure7-4 and Figure 7-5).

Apress®
ONE TWO THREE FOUR
Go!

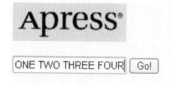

Figure 7-4. *Typing text into the web application*

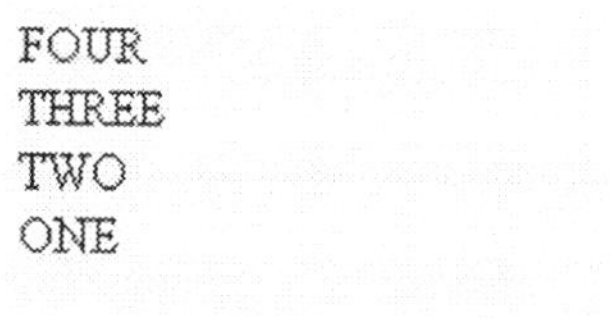
FOUR
THREE
TWO
ONE

Figure 7-5. *The resulting output from the previous figure*

The Networking Application

Create a new BlackBerry application project called Networking. Create the application and main screen classes in the com.beginningblackberry.networking package as follows:

NetworkingApplication.java:

```
package com.beginningblackberry.networking;

import net.rim.device.api.ui.UiApplication;

public class NetworkingApplication extends UiApplication {

    public NetworkingApplication() {
        NetworkingMainScreen scr = new NetworkingMainScreen();
        pushScreen(scr);
    }

    public static void main(String[] args) {
        NetworkingApplication application = new NetworkingApplication();
        application.enterEventDispatcher();
    }
}
```

NetworkingMainScreen.java:

```
package com.beginningblackberry.networking;

import net.rim.device.api.ui.container.MainScreen;

public class NetworkingMainScreen extends MainScreen {
    public NetworkingMainScreen() {
    }
}
```

Some Controls

The first functionality we'll build is the capability to get images and web page text from the Web.

We'll add a few controls here. First, an edit field to enter the URL, and then a couple of fields to display resources that the application fetches: a BitmapField and another new control called RichTextField. Make the following changes to NetworkingMainScreen.java:

```
    private EditField urlField;
    private BitmapField imageOutputField;
    private RichTextField textOutputField;

    public NetworkingMainScreen() {
        setTitle("Networking");
        urlField = new EditField("URL:", "");
        textOutputField = new RichTextField();
        imageOutputField = new BitmapField();

        add(urlField);
```

```
    add(new SeparatorField());
    add(new LabelField("Image retrieved:"));
    add(imageOutputField);
    add(new SeparatorField());
    add(new LabelField("Text retrieved:"));
    add(textOutputField);
}
```

`RichTextField` is a powerful control. It enables you to display a lot of text on multiple lines with built-in line wrapping and different styles for different parts of the text. For this application, we'll take advantage of the multiline and line wrapping capabilities of `RichTextField` to display the text result of the network requests. We need to add a separate `LabelField` because `RichTextField` has no support for a built-in label.

Next, add a menu item and skeleton method to initiate the HTTP request to `NetworkingMainScreen`:

```
private void getURL() {
}

protected void makeMenu(Menu menu, int instance) {
    super.makeMenu(menu, instance);
    menu.add(new MenuItem("Get", 10, 10) {
        public void run() {
            getURL();
        }
    });
}
```

Making an HTTP Connection

Now let's get to the details of how to make the request. First, note one critical issue. Remember back in the early part of the book when we discussed the event thread? That information is important now. When networking on the BlackBerry, always remember the following:

Never perform a network operation on the event thread.

Earlier, we said that it's a bad idea to do anything that can take a lot of time on the event thread because that would have the effect of freezing the user interface, making the user think the application had hung or crashed. In the case of networking, the situation is worse. Depending on the device and configuration, the API often throws an exception if you try to initiate a network connection from the event thread.

The HttpRequestDispatcher Class

We need to create a separate thread for the HTTP request. Do this by creating a new class that extends `java.lang.Thread`. Call the class `HttpRequestDispatcher`:

```
public class HttpRequestDispatcher extends Thread {
    private String url;
    private String method; // GET or POST
    private NetworkingMainScreen screen;

    public HttpRequestDispatcher(String url, String method, NetworkingMainScreen screen)
    {
        this.url = url;
        this.method = method;
        this.screen = screen;
    }

    public void run() {

    }
}
```

Notice we're passing in an instance of the main screen. This is to give us a way to update the screen when a request succeeds or fails. We'll need to add a couple of methods to let us send these notifications. Add the following method skeletons to NetworkingMainScreen. We'll fill them in later:

```
public class NetworkingMainScreen extends MainScreen {
    // ...
    public void requestSucceeded(byte[] result, String contentType) {

    }

    public void requestFailed(String message) {

    }
```

If we wanted to make our HttpRequestDispatcher more general purpose we'd define an interface containing the previous methods for NetworkingMainScreen to implement. Because we're just illustrating basic concepts here, we've elected to use NetworkingMainScreen directly and eliminate the extra java file that an interface would require.

The Run Method

We will perform only GET requests at first. There will be an extra line or two for POST requests. All the work is done in the run method:

```
public void run() {
    try {
        HttpConnection connection = (HttpConnection)Connector.open(url);
        connection.setRequestMethod(method);

        int responseCode = connection.getResponseCode();
        if (responseCode != HttpConnection.HTTP_OK) {
            screen.requestFailed("Unexpected response code: " + responseCode);
            connection.close();
            return;
        }
```

```
        String contentType = connection.getHeaderField("Content-type");
        ByteArrayOutputStream baos = new ByteArrayOutputStream();

        InputStream responseData = connection.openInputStream();
        byte[] buffer = new byte[10000];
        int bytesRead = responseData.read(buffer);
        while(bytesRead > 0) {
            baos.write(buffer, 0, bytesRead);
            bytesRead = responseData.read(buffer);
        }
        baos.close();
        connection.close();

        screen.requestSucceeded(baos.toByteArray(), contentType);
    } catch (IOException ex) {
        screen.requestFailed(ex.toString());
    }
}
```

The first couple of lines set up the connection parameters:

```
        HttpConnection connection = (HttpConnection)Connector.open(url);
        connection.setRequestMethod(method);
```

As mentioned previously, you get an `HttpConnection` back from `Connector.open` only if the URL starts with `http://`. Be sure to type that into the text field when using the application!

At this point in the run method, network activity has not occurred yet. The connection is still in the *setup* state. `HttpConnection` doesn't actually start a connection until you ask for some data that it needs to request from the server. This is useful to remember because there's often a noticeable delay in initiating a network connection, and in this case, it'll happen when the next line is called:

```
        int responseCode = connection.getResponseCode();
```

The response code is just the standard HTTP response code value: 200 if the request succeeded and some other value if it didn't (it's slightly more complicated, but for our purposes, that's fine). Test the response code and if it's not 200 (`HttpConnection.HTTP_OK`), notify the main screen and stop:

```
        if (responseCode != HttpConnection.HTTP_OK) {
            screen.requestFailed("Unexpected response code: " + responseCode);
            connection.close();
            return;
        }
```

Next, retrieve the value of the Content-type response header. Getting a header is another method that would initiate the connection if we hadn't already called `getResponseCode`:

```
        String contentType = connection.getHeaderField("Content-type");
```

Finally, open the connection's input stream and read the data into a buffer. We use a `ByteArrayOutputStream` as a convenient way to buffer the bytes from the input stream:

```
        ByteArrayOutputStream baos = new ByteArrayOutputStream();
```

```
        InputStream responseData = connection.openInputStream();
        byte[] buffer = new byte[10000];
        int bytesRead = responseData.read(buffer);
        while(bytesRead > 0) {
            baos.write(buffer, 0, bytesRead);
            bytesRead = responseData.read(buffer);
        }
        baos.close();
        connection.close();
```

Finally, we pass the data along with the content type back to the main screen to deal with
the following:

```
screen.requestSucceeded(baos.toByteArray(), contentType);
```

Initiating the Connection

The getURL method requires only a couple of lines to initiate the connection:

```
    private void getURL() {
        HttpRequestDispatcher dispatcher = new HttpRequestDispatcher(urlField.getText(),
"GET", this);
        dispatcher.start();
            }
```

Displaying the Response Failed Notification

Now let's start modifying NetworkingMainScreen to handle the results of the HTTP
request. First, we'll have requestFailed display a dialog box when called.

Remember, this method is being called from a different thread than the event thread, so
we can't directly call Dialog.alert. Instead, we'll use UiApplication.invokeLater to let
the event thread display the dialog at the next available opportunity:

```
    public void requestFailed(final String message) {
        UiApplication.getUiApplication().invokeLater(new Runnable() {
            public void run() {
                Dialog.alert("Request failed.  Reason: " + message);
            }
        });
    }
```

> **NOTE:** If you're paying close attention you'll notice one change to the method signature: we
> made the message parameter *final*. This is necessary because we use it inside an anonymous
> inner class (the Runnable that we create). Final just means that we're not allowed to do
> something like this in the body of the requestFailed method:
>
> ```
> message = "";  // ERROR - will not work!
> ```

Testing It

We're now at a stage where we can see a network connection happen: by typing in a URL to a page that doesn't exist, we'll get a failed notification and see a dialog.

Before we run the application in the simulator, there's an additional topic you need to know—the MDS simulator.

The MDS Simulator

By default, the BlackBerry makes connections using the BES/MDS method. To let you test this, the JDE and Eclipse Plug-in include an MDS simulator. This needs to be running to make MDS-enabled connections from your simulator.

Fortunately, running the MDS simulator is easy. In the JDE Plug-in for Eclipse, open your debug configuration, and on the Simulator tab, ensure *Launch Mobile Data System Connection Service (MDS-CS) with simulator* is enabled as shown in Figure 7-6.

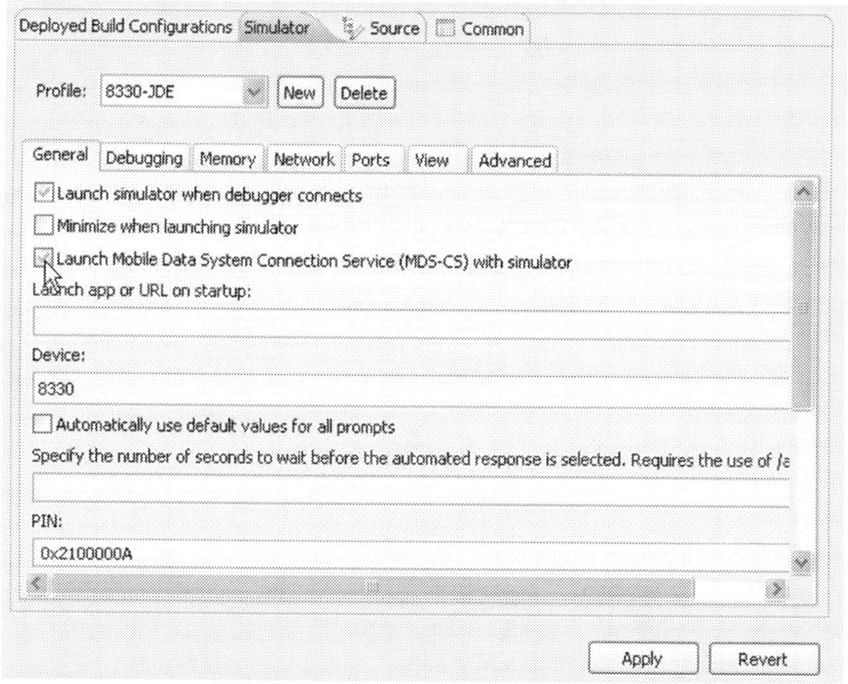

Figure 7-6. *Enabling the MDS simulator from the Eclipse plug-in*

Similarly, from the JDE, open the Preferences dialog and under the Simulator/General tab, select the same option; see Figure 7-7 for the JDE Preferences dialog.

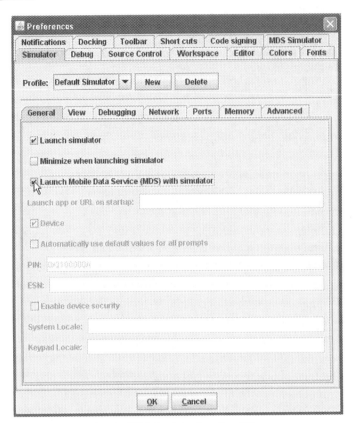

Figure 7-7. *Enabling the MDS simulator from the JDE*

NOTE: Some versions of the JDE use the term MDS and some use MDS-CS. For our purposes, they are the same thing.

Launching the MDS Manually

If you have the standalone JDE installed, you can also launch the MDS simulator from the Start menu. It's common to have to restart the MDS simulator from time to time when debugging your applications; sometimes, it can take a few attempts to get it to connect. If you cannot perform a network connection, simply stop and restart both the MDS and Device simulators. The MDS that comes with the JDE will work fine with the MDS that comes with the JDE Plug-in for Eclipse, so if you have both environments installed, you can run the MDS from the JDE and run your simulator from Eclipse.

Running the Application

Start your debug session. Along with the simulator, you'll see a command prompt window open running the MDS (see Figure 7-8).

```
C:\WINDOWS\system32\cmd.exe                                    _ □ ×
Aug 8, 2009 2:01:48 PM org.apache.catalina.core.ApplicationContext log
INFO: C:\eclipse\plugins\net.rim.eide.componentpack4.7.0_4.7.0.46\components\MDS

Aug 8, 2009 2:01:48 PM org.apache.catalina.core.ApplicationContext log
INFO: AdministrationController <Statistics>:init
Aug 8, 2009 2:01:48 PM org.apache.catalina.core.ApplicationContext log
INFO: C:\eclipse\plugins\net.rim.eide.componentpack4.7.0_4.7.0.46\components\MDS

Aug 8, 2009 2:01:49 PM org.apache.coyote.http11.Http11BaseProtocol init
INFO: Initializing Coyote HTTP/1.1 on http-8080
Aug 8, 2009 2:01:49 PM org.apache.coyote.http11.Http11BaseProtocol start
INFO: Starting Coyote HTTP/1.1 on http-8080
<2009-08-08 14:01:49.218 EDT>:[42]:<MDS-CS_MDS>:<DEBUG>:<LAYER = SCM, Web Server
 Started>
<2009-08-08 14:01:54.218 EDT>:[43]:<MDS-CS_MDS>:<DEBUG>:<LAYER = SCM, EVENT = Ex
pire records from device storage that are expired or older than 0 hours; 0>
<2009-08-08 14:01:54.218 EDT>:[44]:<MDS-CS_MDS>:<DEBUG>:<LAYER = SCM, EVENT = Ex
pire records process ended; 0>
<2009-08-08 14:01:54.281 EDT>:[45]:<MDS-CS_MDS>:<DEBUG>:<LAYER = SCM, EVENT = Ad
min. Task- refresh media management>
<2009-08-08 14:01:54.281 EDT>:[46]:<MDS-CS_MDS>:<DEBUG>:<LAYER = SCM, EVENT = Th
e push service is ready to receive requests>
<2009-08-08 14:01:54.281 EDT>:[47]:<MDS-CS_MDS>:<DEBUG>:<LAYER = SCM, EVENT = Ad
min. Task- pending push messages>
```

Figure 7-8. *The MDS simulator running*

Let's test the requestFailed method by making a request for a page that doesn't exist. Start the application, in the URL field, type http://beginningblackberry.appspot.com/nopage.html, and then open the menu and click Get, as shown in Figure 7-9.

Figure 7-9. *Type a URL to a nonexistent page, and then click Get.*

After a momentary delay, you should see a dialog informing you that the request failed with a response code of 404, which is HTTP speak for "not found," as shown in Figure 7-10.

Figure 7-10. *URL not found*

Believe it or not, this is a good result. The 404 error is sent by the server, meaning we've successfully made a network connection! Next, we'll fill in the details to handle a request for a resource that actually exists.

Handling Successful Requests

We'll do the following things in the requestSucceeded method:

- Check the contentType.
- If the content type is an image (image/png, image/jpeg, image/gif), decode the image and display it.
- If the content type is text (text/plain, text/html, or text/anything), display the text in the RichTextField.
- Otherwise, display an error message.

The code for this is actually simple. Again, this method is called from outside the event thread so you have to be sure to get the event lock before you manipulate the UI:

```
public void requestSucceeded(byte[] result, String contentType) {
        if (contentType.equals("image/png") ||
                    contentType.equals("image/jpeg") ||
```

```
                    contentType.equals("image/gif")) {
    Bitmap bitmap = Bitmap.createBitmapFromBytes(result, 0, result.length, 1);
    synchronized (UiApplication.getEventLock()) {
        imageOutputField.setBitmap(bitmap);
                            }

    }
    else if (contentType.startsWith("text/")) {
            String strResult = new String(result);
            synchronized (UiApplication.getEventLock()) {
                    textOutputField.setText(strResult);
            }
    }
    else {
            synchronized (UiApplication.getEventLock()) {
                    Dialog.alert("Unknown content type: " + contentType);
            }
    }
}
```

Everything is straightforward. The only thing to note is that we used three separate synchronized blocks instead of making the entire method synchronized. Generally, this is a good UI programming principle. We minimize the amount of work done in the synchronized blocks so we can minimize the impact to the user experience. In this case, it probably wouldn't be noticeable, but if we encoded or scaling scaled a very large image or large amount of text, putting all that into the synchronized block would lock up the event thread for longer.

Try It

Now, run the application again. First, try the URL for the main test web application: http://beginningblackberry.appspot.com. Enter the URL, and in the menu, click Get. You should see a lot of HTML in the text area, such as what you see in Figure 7-11.

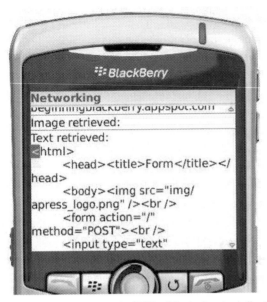

Figure 7-11. *Retrieving the HTML of the test web application*

When we opened an HttpConnection to http://beginningblackberry.appspot.com, the server sent back "text/html" as the content type, so the method interpreted the data as a string and put the text into the RichTextField. Now let's verify that the code for retrieving an image works, too. Because you can see the URL to the apress_logo image in the HTML—img/apress_logo.png—you just need to add that to the end of the URL to get http://beginningblackberry.appspot.com/img/apress_logo.png. Then, select Get again and you'll see a result like what you see in Figure 7-12.

Figure 7-12. *Retrieving the logo from the web application*

In this case, the server sent back image/png as the content-type, so the code interpreted the data from the input stream as the bytes for an image and successfully decoded and displayed it.

Two-Way Interaction: Sending Data via HTTP POST

Now we'll complete our exploration of HTTP using the BlackBerry by sending some data to the web application using an HTTP POST. Remember that the web application takes a series of words separated by spaces and returns the same list of words in reverse order but separated by new lines and HTML break (br) tags.

How an HTML Form Works

You might already know this, but let's review how a POST from an HTML form in a browser works. We will duplicate this functionality in the Networking application.

The web application contains this HTML:

```
<form action="/" method="POST"><br />
        <input type="text" name="content"></input>
        <input type="submit" value="Go!"/>
</form>
```

This defines a form that the browser uses to send data to the web application. Specifically, the first line says to send the data via HTTP POST to the URL "/," which is just the base URL of the web application.

The input type="submit" defines the Go button as the button that invokes the POST.

Finally, the input type="text" line defines the text box and gives it the name content. The web application expects the body of the POST request to contain something like the following:

```
content=ONE+TWO+THREE
```

The "+" characters are a way of encoding spaces in the input. We have to do this, too. In addition, the content type header in the request to the server should be application/x-www-form-urlencoded to indicate that the content is encoded in this way.

Modifying HttpRequestDispatcher

Most of the code to perform a POST is the same as to perform a GET, so we'll just modify the run method of HttpRequestDispatcher to handle both. First, we need a way to pass the POST body to HttpRequestDispatcher. Create a new member variable called postData and a new constructor so we can initialize it:

```
private byte[] postData;

public HttpRequestDispatcher(String url, String method,
                NetworkingMainScreen screen, byte[] postData) {
        this.url = url;
```

```
        this.method = method;
        this.screen = screen;
        this.postData = postData;
}
```

Next, we need to check if we have post data to send before initiating the connection. If we do, we'll set the content-type header by using `HttpConnection.setRequestProperty`, and then open an output stream for the connection and write the data. Modify the run method by adding the following lines:

```
if (method.equals("POST") && postData != null) {
        connection.setRequestProperty("Content-type", "application/x-
www-form-urlencoded");

        OutputStream requestOutput = connection.openOutputStream();
        requestOutput.write(postData);
        requestOutput.close();
}
```

Everything else should stay the same. We'll handle the response the same way by calling `requestSucceeded` in `NetworkingMainScreen`.

Modifying NetworkingMainScreen

We need two things in our screen: an edit field to enter the post data and a way to invoke the Post request (a menu item and method).

Add the edit field first. Declare a new EditField called postDataField:

```
private EditField postDataField;
```

Then, initialize it and position it right below the URL field:

```
add(urlField);
add(new SeparatorField());

postDataField = new EditField("Post data:", "");
add(postDataField);
add(new SeparatorField());

add(new LabelField("Image retrieved:"));
add(imageOutputField);
```

Next, define the postURL method. It does the same thing as the getURL method with the additional functionality of taking the text from the post data edit field and encoding it for the body of the post. We'll use the class `net.rim.blackberry.api.browser.URLEncodedPostData` to do the actual encoding and formatting of the data for the request body:

```
private void postURL() {
        String postString = postDataField.getText();
        URLEncodedPostData encodedData = new URLEncodedPostData(null, false);
        encodedData.append("content", postString);
        HttpRequestDispatcher dispatcher = new HttpRequestDispatcher(urlField
                        .getText(), "POST", this, encodedData.getBytes());
        dispatcher.start();
}
```

If postDataField contains the text "A B C", the byte[] output from encodedData will be "content=A+B+C".

Adding the menu item is exactly the same as the Get menu item. Add the following lines to makeMenu:

```
menu.add(new MenuItem("Post", 10, 10) {
        public void run() {
                postURL();
        }
});
```

We're done. We don't need to make modifications to requestSucceeded because we want the same functionality, which is to display the text.

Let's try it out. Enter http://beginningblackberry.appspot.com in the URL field and ONE TWO THREE FOUR FIVE in the Post data field, and then click Post from the menu. You should see the words, one per line, in the output as shown in Figure 7-13.

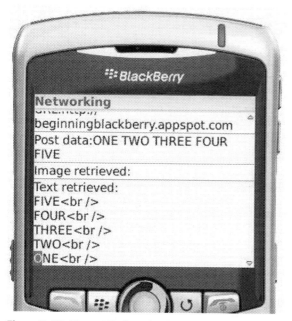

Figure 7-13. *The result of posting ONE TWO THREE FOUR FIVE*

Making Secure HTTP (HTTPS) Connections

To make a connection to a secure HTTP server, replace http:// with https:// in the Connector.open method. Fortunately, the web application also supports HTTPS connections, so simply substitute https:// into the URL to make https://beginningblackberry.appspot.com, and then click Get. The result will look almost the same as the non-secure HTTP connection (see Figure 7-14).

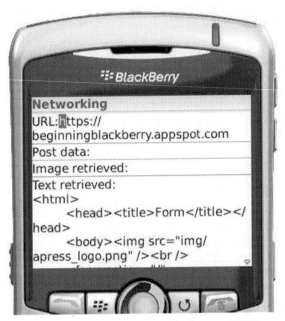

Figure 7-14. *Retrieving the web application over HTTPS*

Performing the POST works in a similar way. We haven't had to change the connection-handling code because `Connector.open` returns an `HttpsConnection` instead of `HttpConnection`, and `HttpsConnection` derives from `HttpConnection`. We can, however, detect this and display some information about the connection (in this case, the issuer of the TLS certificate). Add the following lines to the run method of `HttpRequestDispatcher` right after getting the response code:

```
if (connection instanceof HttpsConnection) {
        HttpsConnection secureConnection = (HttpsConnection)connection;
        final String issuer =
secureConnection.getSecurityInfo().getServerCertificate().getIssuer();
        UiApplication.getUiApplication().invokeLater(new Runnable() {
                public void run() {
                        Dialog.inform("Secure Connection, certificate
issued by: " + issuer);
                }
        }
}
```

Now, if we enter the `https://` URL, we'll get a dialog with some info as shown in Figure 7-15.

Figure 7-15. *Information about the security of the connection*

NOTE: Something to be aware of with HTTPS connections—and this applies to secure socket (TLS and SSL) connections, too—is that things are simple only when the certificate provided by the server is known to the BlackBerry, or, in the case of a BES/MDS connection, known to the BES. In the case of an unknown certificate such as a self-signed certificate, a prompt is displayed to the user asking them to verify the connection. If the connection is a BES/MDS connection, this prompt is displayed only if certificate verification is done on the device by adding the EndToEndRequired=true parameter to the end of the URL to force certificate verification to happen on the device. Otherwise, the connection just fails. If you stick with certificates from known certification authorities, you shouldn't have to worry about any of this.

Summary: HTTP Networking

You've learned the basics of HTTP networking, and created an application that performed both an HTTP GET and HTTP POST. The application performed the requests in a separate thread, which is necessary for all BlackBerry networking. We decoded the responses by first looking at the Content-type header to determine what the server was sending back, and then decoding either an image or text data. We also encoded our POST request body and set the Content-type header for the request appropriately. Finally, we peformed an HTTPS connection simply by switching the scheme of the URL, and using the HttpsConnection interface got some information about the connection.

Connection Method: Using Direct TCP/IP Instead of BES/MDS

Now, let's take a few minutes to see how to force a connection to make a direct TCP/IP connection to the server instead of using the BES/MDS. The Networking application currently uses the device's default connection method. As mentioned earlier, if you run the application on a device that's not activated on a BES, the requests will already go over direct TCP/IP. However, if you run on a device connected to a BES, the POST and GET requests are done through the BES. To force them to go directly, we just have to add a BlackBerry-specific parameter to the end of the URL when we call `Connector.open`. The parameter we want is `;deviceside=true`, so the URL for the web application becomes:

```
http://b eginningblackberry.appspot.com;deviceside=true
```

Modify the run method of `HttpRequestDispatcher` to add this automatically:

```
HttpConnection connection = (HttpConnection)Connector.open(url + ";deviceside=true");
```

We can actually test this on the simulator because it respects this parameter, too. If we specify `deviceside=true`, the simulator won't connect through the MDS simulator. So, uncheck the appropriate Launch Mobile Data System check box, ensure the MDS command window isn't open (if it is, just close it), and then run the application again. We'll be able to make connections without the MDS simulator running!

Making a Connection Using WAP 2.0

I mentioned that WAP 2.0 was a better choice than direct TCP/IP because of configuration issues. It's a little more difficult to use, as it requires an extra parameter at the end of the URL that includes the UID of the service record for the WAP 2.0 protocol. We'll start by creating a method in `HttpRequestDispatcher` to find this service book.

The WAP 2.0 service book record has a CID of WPTCP, but this CID is used for a few other connection methods, so the recommended algorithm for finding the correct record is to look for a record with a CID of WPTCP and a UID that doesn't contain WIFI or MMS.

First, add the following imports to the top of the file to get access to the service book-related classes:

```
import net.rim.device.api.servicebook.ServiceBook;
import net.rim.device.api.servicebook.ServiceRecord;
```

The code for the method follows:

```
private ServiceRecord getWAP2ServiceRecord() {
    ServiceBook sb = ServiceBook.getSB();
    ServiceRecord[] records = sb.getRecords();

    for(int i = 0; i < records.length; i++) {
        String cid = records[i].getCid().toLowerCase();
        String uid = records[i].getUid().toLowerCase();
```

```
      if (cid.indexOf("wptcp") != -1 &&
            uid.indexOf("wifi") == -1 &&
            uid.indexOf("mms") == -1) {
        return records[i];
      }
    }
    return null;
}
```

If a matching service record isn't found, WAP 2.0 isn't configured on the device, and the method will return null. In that case, default back to a direct TCP/IP connection. Otherwise, we'll add the parameter ConnectionUID=<UID of the record> to indicate that we want to connect using WAP 2.0. Modify the code in the run method of HttpRequestDispatcher as follows:

```
ServiceRecord record = getWAP2ServiceRecord();
  String connectionParameters = ";deviceside=true";
  if (record != null) {
    connectionParameters += ";ConnectionUID=" + record.getUid();
  }
  HttpConnection connection = (HttpConnection)Connector.open(url +
connectionParameters);
```

Making a Connection Using BIS

What about using the BIS connection method described at the beginning of this chapter? Applications are approved to use BIS to connect on a case-by-case basis, but you have to be a member of the BlackBerry Alliance Program to get access. Generally, the BlackBerry Alliance Program is good to get involved with as an independent software vendor for BlackBerry. More information about the Alliance Program is available at:

http://na.blackberry.com/eng/partners/alliance.jsp

For those reasons, making a connection using BIS is outside the scope of this book, but if you understand the basics of connecting using BES/MDS and direct TCP/IP, you shouldn't have any trouble connecting over BIS.

Making a WiFi Connection

Connecting via WiFi is easy if the device has been configured to use a WiFi access point.

Remember, if your application is used on a device that's activated on a BES, and you're using the BES/MDS or default connection method, your connection is made over WiFi as per the device configuration.

To explicitly force a direct WiFi connection, append the parameter ;interface=wifi to the end of the connection string. For example, modify the connector call to be:

```
    HttpConnection connection = (HttpConnection)Connector.open(url +
";interface=wifi");
```

Note that this bypasses any other wireless network connection method, so if the device is not within range of an appropriate WiFi access point, the connection will fail.

Determining Network Availabilty

We've covered how to make network connections through various methods, but how do you determine which ones you can use? There are a couple of classes in the BlackBerry API that provide an easy way to do this.

Using CoverageInfo

The net.rim.device.api.system.CoverageInfo class enables you to determine which connection methods are currently available to the BlackBerry device. It looks at the device's radio, current network coverage, and service book, and it provides information about what types of network connections are possible.

The API for this class has changed somewhat between OS 4.2 and OS 4.5. We'll cover the OS 4.5 version.

The main method to determine coverage is the getCoverageStatus method. The no-parameter form of this method returns a bitmask of the different connection methods available over all physical network types (usually mobile network and WiFi, but also Bluetooth and USB connections to the computer if applicable). For example, if we called the method in an area with full network coverage on a device that's activated on a BES and with a wireless service plan that allows direct TCP/IP access, we'd expect getCoverageStatus to return COVERAGE_MDS | COVERAGE_DIRECT | COVERAGE_BIS_B

Note that the different COVERAGE values can each indicate several types of available connection methods:

- COVERAGE_MDS means you can make connections using the BES/MDS connection method.
- COVERAGE_DIRECT means you can make conections using direct TCP/IP or WAP.
- COVERAGE_BIS_B means you can make connections using BIS.

Using WLANInfo

The net.rim.device.api.system.WLANInfo class, available in OS 4.3 and later, lets you determine if you can make a direct WiFi connection.

Usage of the class is easy. If the getWLANState method returns WLANInfo.WLAN_STATE_CONNECTED, then the device's WiFi is turned on and connected to a wireless access point, and you can make direct WiFi connections.

Putting It All Together

We'll modify our run method one last time to use CoverageInfo and WLANInfo to determine which connection methods are available and connect in our preferred order. For our application, we'll look for available connection methods in the following order:

- WiFi
- WAP 2.0
- BES/MDS
- Direct TCP/IP

We've left out BIS because it's only available to approved applications, and we left out WAP 1.0 because it's generally not recommended.

Before we proceed with the code, remember to add the imports for WLANInfo and CoverageInfo to the top of HttpRequestDispatcher.java:

```
import net.rim.device.api.system.CoverageInfo;
import net.rim.device.api.system.WLANInfo;
```

The new connection code for HttpRequestDispatcher's run method to attempt connections in the given order follows:

```
        String connectionParameters = "";
        if (WLANInfo.getWLANState() == WLANInfo.WLAN_STATE_CONNECTED) {
            // Connected to a WiFi access point
            connectionParameters = ";interface=wifi";
        } else {
            int coverageStatus = CoverageInfo.getCoverageStatus();
            ServiceRecord record = getWAP2ServiceRecord();
            if (record != null
                    && (coverageStatus & CoverageInfo.COVERAGE_DIRECT) ==
                    CoverageInfo.COVERAGE_DIRECT) {
                // Have network coverage and a WAP 2.0 service book record
                connectionParameters = ";deviceside=true;ConnectionUID="
                    + record.getUid();
        } else if ((coverageStatus & CoverageInfo.COVERAGE_MDS) ==
                CoverageInfo.COVERAGE_MDS) {
            // Have an MDS service book and network coverage
            connectionParameters = ";deviceside=false";
        } else if ((coverageStatus & CoverageInfo.COVERAGE_DIRECT) ==
                CoverageInfo.COVERAGE_DIRECT) {
            // Have network coverage but no WAP 2.0 service book record
            connectionParameters = ";deviceside=true";
        }
```

The previous code will work with JDE 4.5 and higher. This is because of the use of CoverageInfo.COVERAGE_DIRECT, which replaced CoverageInfo.COVERAGE_CARRIER from JDE 4.5 and above. You can, however, make the code compile in all versions of the JDE 4.3 and higher by replacing CoverageInfo.COVERAGE_DIRECT with its constant value of 1, which is the same value that is used for CoverageInfo.COVERAGE_CARRIER in earlier JDE versions.

Notice that we have to check the service book to know if we should attempt a WAP 2.0 connection because CoverageInfo tells us only that the device has network coverage to the carrier, but CoverageInfo by itself can tell us if the device is able to connect via BES/MDS. It's able to check both the network coverage and service book status.

If you have a BlackBerry device that is WiFi capable, try running it with different combinations of WiFi and mobile network settings, such as turning either WiFi or the mobile network on or off.. You should be able to connect in a variety of configurations.

TCP Socket Connections

Some applications require a lower level of network access than HTTP provides. For example, connecting to a streaming media server, FTP server, or any other non-web server requires a lower level of network access than HTTP provides. In these cases, you can open a TCP socket in much the same way as an HTTP connection by substituting socket:// for http:// - or ssl:// or tls:// for a secure connection.

A Simple Socket Application

We'll make some simple modifications to the Networking application to perform an HTTP GET using a socket connection instead of the HTTP connection functionality. Because the mechanics are so similar to HTTP connections, and this is a simple (and somewhat contrived) example, we'll go fairly quickly.

Create a new class to perform socket connections. This is analogous to HttpRequestDispatcher but uses SocketConnection instead. We'll present the code and then discuss it:

```java
package com.beginningblackberry.networking;

import java.io.ByteArrayOutputStream;
import java.io.IOException;
import java.io.InputStream;
import java.io.OutputStream;

import javax.microedition.io.Connector;
import javax.microedition.io.SocketConnection;

public class SocketConnector extends Thread {
    private String host;
    private NetworkingMainScreen screen;

    public SocketConnector(String host, NetworkingMainScreen screen) {
        this.host = host;
        this.screen = screen;
    }

    public void run() {
        try {
```

```
            SocketConnection connection =
(SocketConnection)Connector.open("socket://" + host + ":80");
            OutputStream out = connection.openOutputStream();
            InputStream in = connection.openInputStream();
            String request = "GET / HTTP/1.1\r\n" +
            "Host:" + host + "\r\n" +
            "\r\n" +
            "\r\n";
            out.write(request.getBytes());
            out.flush();
            ByteArrayOutputStream baos = new ByteArrayOutputStream();

            int firstByte = in.read();
            if (firstByte >= 0) {
                    baos.write((byte)firstByte);
                    int bytesAvailable = in.available();
                    while(bytesAvailable > 0) {
                            byte[] buffer = new byte[bytesAvailable];
                            in.read(buffer);
                            baos.write(buffer);
                            bytesAvailable = in.available();
                    }
            }
            baos.close();
            connection.close();

            screen.requestSucceeded(baos.toByteArray(), "text/plain");
        } catch (IOException ex) {
            screen.requestFailed(ex.getMessage());
        }
    }

}
```

Along with the screen parameter to let us write output, we're passing in a host. We use this to open the socket connection to port 80, the usual web server port, and to construct the HTTP request because a Host header is required by the HTTP protocol.

> **NOTE:** that you should always specify a port number when opening a socket connection. HTTP connections default to port 80, and HTTPS to port 443, but there's no concept of a "default" port for a socket connection.

The HTTP request is constructed according to the HTTP protocol specification. we write only the Host header, as it's the only required one.

The first step in reading the response from the socket is this line:

```
int firstByte = in.read();
```

This lets us wait for the server to write the first byte of the response back to the socket. Remember, at the socket level, there's no built-in concept of request-response. The server can theoretically write back at any point or wait any length of time before writing data, so we have to wait and check that the first value we get is not –1, which indicates the server has closed the connection.

We then read only as long as bytes are available. In this case, we know the behavior of the server—that it'll write the entire response as one chunk. In other cases, `InputStream.available()` tells you only the number of bytes currently available to be read back. More bytes might be available after you've finished reading the initial number returned by available.

Adding Socket Support to the Main Screen

To give access to the TCP socket functionality from the main screen, we'll have the URL field double as a hostname field, so no changes are required to the onscreen controls, just an additional menu item.

Add the following lines to makeMenu:

```
menu.add(new MenuItem("Socket Get", 10, 10) {
        public void run() {
                socketGet();
        }
});
```

Add the following method to NetworkingMainScreen:

```
private void socketGet() {
        SocketConnector connector = new SocketConnector(urlField.getText(), this);
        connector.start();
}
```

Testing It

Because we're back to using an MDS connection, remember to enable the MDS in the simulator debug options (or run it from the Start menu). Run the application again and in the URL field, type `beginningblackberry.appspot.com`. Don't type a scheme portion for the URL. (See Figure 7-15.) Then, in the menu, click Socket Get:

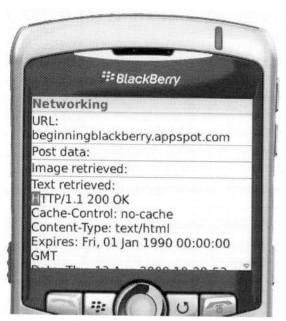

Figure 7-15. *Retrieving the web application's main page using a TCP socket*

We're displaying the raw HTTP request, not just the body portion. If you scroll down, you'll see the same data as we got with the HTTP GET.

Summary

In this chapter, we threw open the doors of the BlackBerry handheld and built an application that could talk to the world. We discussed the various networking options available to BlackBerry devices and the connection framework that makes them all available.

We started by building an application that used the HTTP connection framework to talk to a web application by retrieving HTML and images and sending data back to the application. We then saw how it was easy to extend this to a secure connection using HTTPS.

Finally, we briefly explored TCP sockets by retrieving the web application's main page over a TCP socket connection without going through the BlackBerry platform's HTTP layer.

The examples here have all been fairly simple, but if you worked through them and understood them, you have the knowledge to create most kinds of network-ready BlackBerry applications.

At this point, you've seen enough of the BlackBerry API to create a wide range of useful applications. The next chapter deals with something less general, but still extremely valuable for a growing number of application types — location-based services. We finish by talking about how you can package and distribute your applications. So take a deep breath, we're almost done!

Chapter **8**

Where Am I? Using Location-Based Services

The BlackBerry API includes functionality to determine where in the world your device is and information such as the speed of the device. This information is obtained using the Global Positioning System (GPS) hardware that's built in to many current devices, or it is obtained optionally from an external Bluetooth GPS receiver.

In addition, the BlackBerry device includes a mapping application called BlackBerry Maps with an API that applications can call to show a map opened to any location in the world, routes from location to location, and points of interest on a map.

In OS 4.5 and higher, you can embed a map in your appliction's user interface as a control, giving you more power over how you use BlackBerry Maps.

Location-based services can help you create compelling applications for BlackBerry, but you must be aware of the limitations in device and OS support for various types of functionality.

In this chapter, we build an application that lets you explore all aspects of location-based services. You start by simply retrieving the device's location using the GPS functionality, you will move on to explore BlackBerry Maps, you learn how to launch the application from your application, and then you mark your device's position (or any coordinates) on a map. Finally, we discuss embedding a map control in your application's user interface.

GPS Support on BlackBerry Devices

The Location API for retrieving device latitude and longitude has been available on BlackBerry since OS 4.0.2. Although all devices running OS 4.2 and later support an external Bluetooth GPS receiver, at the time of writing, GPS was built in to only the following devices (the list includes devices from the 8100 Pearl and later):

BlackBerry Pearl 8110

BlackBerry Pearl 8130

BlackBerry Curve 8310

BlackBerry Curve 8330

BlackBerry Curve 8350i

BlackBerry Pearl Flip 8230

BlackBerry 8800

BlackBerry 8820

BlackBerry 8830

BlackBerry Bold

BlackBerry Storm

BlackBerry Curve 8900

BlackBerry Tour

For the most up-to-date list, visit `http://www.blackberry.com`.

The device's preferred source for GPS information—the internal GPS hardware or an external GPS receiver—is configured by the user. The location API uses whichever source is configured to provide information.

The Location API

The BlackBerry uses the Java ME Location API to get location information, such as latitude, longitude, altitude, speed, and course (direction). This package is located in `javax.microedition.location`.

GPS Modes

You can use GPS in three main modes: Cell Site, Assisted GPS, and Unassisted GPS. All are supported by any device that supports GPS (or has an external GPS receiver) though Assisted GPS can only be used where the wireless network supports it. These modes are discussed in the following sections.

Cell Site

The Cell Site mode determines the location of the device solely based on cell tower locations and signal strengths. This provides only location, not speed or other route information. The accuracy is generally poor. Unlike the real GPS methods, it is almost instantaneous.

Assisted GPS

Assisted GPS uses GPS hardware and assistance from the wireless network to do things such as locate the GPS satellites to speed up the satellite acquisition and location process. Generally, this provides high accuracy, and although it is slower than Cell Site location, it is faster than Unassisted GPS location.

Unassisted GPS

Unassisted GPS uses only the GPS hardware for location. This provides a high degree of accuracy, but it might take two minutes or longer to acquire satellite signals and determine the device's location. Of course, it works whether there is wireless network coverage available to the device or not.

Specifying a GPS Mode

GPS modes are specified using the `javax.microedition.location.Criteria` class, which enables you to specify the requirements for the location provider. You create an instance of the `Criteria` class and pass it into `javax.microedition.location.LocationProvider.getInstance`. Based on your requirements, the BlackBerry then chooses the appropriate location mode.

The BlackBerry Javadocs provide a chart telling you which values determine which mode is used, but it's helpful to understand what some of the main criteria mean and why they affect location mode. This is discussed in the following sections.

Longitudinal and Latidunal Accuracy

These are specified in metres: horizontal for longitude and vertical for latitude. Cell Site location is the least accurate; Assisted GPS and Unassisted GPS are both accurate:

```
criteria.setHorizontalAccuracy(accuracy);
criteria.setVerticalAccuracy(accuracy);
```

If any value is specified for these, Cell Site location is ruled out.

Power Consumption

Specifies the maximum allowable power consumption for location. Cell Site mode requires the lowest power, Assisted GPS requires the highest, and Unassisted GPS is somewhere between them:

```
criteria.setPreferredPowerConsumption(Criteria.POWER_USAGE_HIGH);
```

Altitude and Speed and Course

Cell Site location cannot provide either of these, so setting either to true rules it out:

```
criteria.setAltitudeRequired(true);

criteria.setSpeedAndCourseRequired(true);
```

Cost

Because Assisted GPS and Cell Site location use wireless networking, data cost might be associated with each. Unassisted GPS doesn't use the wireless network, so there's no chance that the user can incur additional costs by using location services, so not allowing cost means that Unassisted GPS is the
only choice:

```
criteria.setCostAllowed(true);
```

With all of these interacting criteria, there are several ways to select each of the location modes; the following sections provide an example of criteria that will result in each mode being selected.

To Use Cell Site Location

With this criteria, accuracy is not required, cost is allowed, and preferred power consumption is low:

```
Criteria criteria = new Criteria();
criteria.setHorizontalAccuracy(Criteria.NO_REQUIREMENT);
criteria.setVerticalAccuracy(Criteria.NO_REQUIREMENT);
criteria.setCostAllowed(true);
criteria.setPreferredPowerConsumption(Criteria.POWER_USAGE_LOW);
```

To Use Assisted GPS Location

With this criteria, accuracy is not required, cost is allowed, and preferred power consumption is medium:

```
Criteria criteria = new Criteria();
criteria.setHorizontalAccuracy(Criteria.NO_REQUIREMENT);
criteria.setVerticalAccuracy(Criteria.NO_REQUIREMENT);
criteria.setCostAllowed(true);
criteria.setPreferredPowerConsumption(Criteria.POWER_USAGE_MEDIUM);
```

To Use Assisted and Unassisted Modes

With this criteria, the initial location is retrieved using Assisted GPS; subsequent locations are fully unassisted:

Accuracy is 50 metres, cost is allowed, and preferred power consumption is high:

```
Criteria criteria = new Criteria();
criteria.setHorizontalAccuracy(50);
criteria.setVerticalAccuracy(50);
criteria.setCostAllowed(true);
criteria.setPreferredPowerConsumption(Criteria.POWER_USAGE_HIGH);
```

To Use Only Unassisted Mode

Unassisted GPS is used for the first and all subsequent location retrievals.

Accuracy is 50 meters, cost is not allowed, and power consumption is high or at no requirement:

```
Criteria criteria = new Criteria();
criteria.setHorizontalAccuracy(50);
criteria.setVerticalAccuracy(50);
criteria.setCostAllowed(false);
criteria.setPreferredPowerConsumption(Criteria.POWER_USAGE_HIGH);
```

The Location Application

Now let's put all this knowledge to use and create an application that uses the location API.

As you should expect by now, you'll start by creating a new BlackBerry CLDC application. Call it Location. Create a main application class and a main screen class called LocationApp and LocationMainScreen, respectively; both are in the com.beginningblackberry.location package. You'll add a few fields to LocationMainScreen, a menu item to update the location, and a skeleton update method. The initial versions of the classes are as follows:

```
package com.beginningblackberry.location;

import net.rim.device.api.ui.UiApplication;

public class LocationApp extends UiApplication {
        public LocationApp() {
                LocationMainScreen screen = new LocationMainScreen();
                pushScreen(screen);
        }

        public static void main(String[] args) {
                LocationApp app = new LocationApp();
                app.enterEventDispatcher();
        }
}
```

LocationMainScreen.java:

```java
package com.beginningblackberry.location;

import net.rim.device.api.ui.MenuItem;
import net.rim.device.api.ui.component.LabelField;
import net.rim.device.api.ui.component.Menu;
import net.rim.device.api.ui.UiApplication;
import net.rim.device.api.ui.component.RichTextField;
import net.rim.device.api.ui.container.HorizontalFieldManager;
import net.rim.device.api.ui.container.MainScreen;


public class LocationMainScreen extends MainScreen {

        private LabelField latitudeLabel;
        private LabelField longitudeLabel;
        private RichTextField messageField;

        public LocationMainScreen() {
                HorizontalFieldManager latManager = new HorizontalFieldManager();
                latManager.add(new LabelField("Latitude:"));
                latitudeLabel = new LabelField("");
                latManager.add(latitudeLabel);

                add(latManager);

                HorizontalFieldManager longManager = new HorizontalFieldManager();
                longManager.add(new LabelField("Longitude:"));
                longitudeLabel = new LabelField("");
                longManager.add(longitudeLabel);

                add(longManager);

                messageField = new RichTextField();
                add(messageField);
        }


        private void update() {
        }

        protected void makeMenu(Menu menu, int instance) {
                super.makeMenu(menu, instance);
                menu.add(new MenuItem("Update", 10, 10) {
                        public void run() {
                                update();
                        }
                });
        }


}
```

Using the location API is another one of those things; like networking, it must be done outside the UI thread. The reason should be clear: getting a fix on GPS satellites can take some time, so the UI thread shouldn't be locked up.

Follow a similar pattern to the Networking example and create a new class to handle the details of working with the location API. First, add a couple of methods to LocationMainScreen to enable the new class to display results to the screen. Add the following to LocationMainScreen:

```
public void setLocation(double longitude, double latitude) {
        synchronized(UiApplication.getEventLock()) {
                longitudeLabel.setText(Double.toString(longitude));
                latitudeLabel.setText(Double.toString(latitude));
        }
}

public void setMessage(String message) {
        synchronized (UiApplication.getEventLock()) {
                messageField.setText(message);

        }
}
```

Location coordinates, as you might have guessed, are returned as double values representing the degrees of longitude and latitude. The message area gives you a freeform spot to print some other interesting information, such as the location method that was actually used and the accuracy of the results.

Create a class called LocationHandler that extends Thread. It will contain an instance of LocationMainScreen so it can update the UI:

```
package com.beginningblackberry.location;

public class LocationHandler extends Thread {
        private LocationMainScreen screen;

        public LocationHandler(LocationMainScreen screen) {
                this.screen = screen;
        }

        public void run() {
        }

}
```

It's time to start using the location API. Add the following imports to the top of LocationHandler.java:

```
import javax.microedition.location.Criteria;
import javax.microedition.location.Location;
import javax.microedition.location.LocationException;
import javax.microedition.location.LocationProvider;
import javax.microedition.location.QualifiedCoordinates;
```

Now you fill in the run method. Basically you fill in the criteria as described earlier (use the Assisted GPS / Unassisted GPS hybrid) and get an instance of `LocationProvider` that you can then use to obtain an actual location. The code is fairly self-explanatory; we present it here and then discuss it:

```
public void run() {
    Criteria criteria = new Criteria();
    criteria.setVerticalAccuracy(50);
    criteria.setHorizontalAccuracy(50);
    criteria.setCostAllowed(true);
    criteria.setPreferredPowerConsumption(
     Criteria.POWER_USAGE_HIGH);

    try {
        screen.setMessage("Getting location...");
        LocationProvider provider =
                LocationProvider.getInstance(criteria);
        Location location = provider.getLocation(-1);

        QualifiedCoordinates qualifiedCoordinates =
         location.getQualifiedCoordinates();

        screen.setLocation(qualifiedCoordinates.getLongitude(),
         qualifiedCoordinates.getLatitude());

        String message = "Successfully got location, method:";
        int method = location.getLocationMethod();
        if ((method & Location.MTA_ASSISTED) ==
         Location.MTA_ASSISTED) {
            message += " Assisted GPS";
        }
        if ((method & Location.MTA_UNASSISTED) ==
         Location.MTA_UNASSISTED) {
            message += " Unassisted GPS";
        }
        if ((method & Location.MTE_CELLID) ==
         Location.MTE_CELLID) {
            message += " Cell Site";
        }

        message += "\nHorizontal (Longitude) Accuracy: ";

        message += qualifiedCoordinates.getHorizontalAccuracy();

        message += "\nVertical (Latitude) Accuracy: ";

        message += qualifiedCoordinates.getVerticalAccuracy();
        screen.setMessage(message);
    } catch (LocationException e) {
        screen.setMessage("LocationException: " +
         e.getMessage());
    } catch (InterruptedException e) {
        screen.setMessage("InterruptedException: " +
         e.getMessage());
    }
}
```

The location method is determined by the criteria that you have specified. In this case, you'd expect it to be Assisted GPS based on the discussion earlier.

We've specified -1 as the parameter to `LocationProvider.getLocation`. This is the timeout parameter in milliseconds. -1 means you use the default for that provider.

The Location you receive is *qualified*; that is, there's some degree of error associated with it, represented by the accuracy values in the `QualifiedCoordinates` class. GPS coordinates will always be qualitifed. The unqualified `Coordinates` class is used mainly to specify coordinates that you want plotted on a map.

Finally, don't forget to fill out the update method in `LocationMainScreen`:

```
private void update() {
    LocationHandler handler = new LocationHandler(this);
    handler.start();
}
```

Now start the simulator or load on to your device and give it a try.

NOTE: that if you're running on the simulator, you can simulate a GPS location from the Simulate ➤ GPS Location menu. Click Update, and you should see your current latitude and longitude.

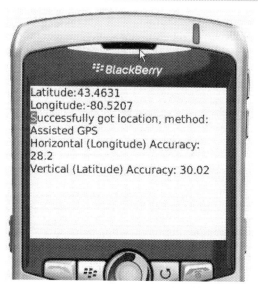

Figure 8-1. *Getting the device's location using Assisted GPS*

Feel free to substitute some of the other criteria values from the previous location modes section to see how they affect things. You should notice that Cell Site location is much quicker than a GPS mode, but generally doesn't have nearly as good accuracy. In many applications, a good approach is to get a rough idea of the user's location using the Cell Site mode, and then refine it using GPS if and when it's available.

Getting Periodic Location Updates Using LocationListener

The location API provides a method to receive regular updates of the device's location using the LocationListener interface. You specify an interval to receive notifications at and a maximum age parameter to indicate how recent the location results must be. Setting a maximum age enables the device to re-use previous location information from the GPS provider. Establishing a GPS location uses processor power and battery life (and potentially network data), so you should specify maximum age as large as possible to help the user's device run efficiently.

You will add support for periodic updates to your application.

Because you want essentially the same functionality for an automatic location update as for a manual location update, you need LocationHandler to act as the LocationListener and move some code around.

First, add an import for LocationListener and change the signature of LocationListener to implement the interface. Also add a boolean flag to indicate whether you want to register for periodic location updates and a constructor to initialize the flag. So you can see your coordinates update, add one more thing, a Vector to store a list of the coordinates, so you can display the distance between location updates:

```
import java.util.Vector;
import javax.microedition.location.LocationListener;

//...

public class LocationHandler extends Thread implements LocationListener {
        private LocationMainScreen screen;
        private boolean periodicUpdates;
        private Vector coordinateHistory = new Vector();

        public LocationHandler(LocationMainScreen screen, boolean update) {
                this.screen = screen;
                this.periodicUpdates = update;
        }
```

LocationListener includes two methods: providerStateChanged, which is invoked whenever the availability of the provider specified by the location criteria changes (for example, if GPS coverage is lost) and locationUpdated, which gives us the actual location updates. For this application you'll provide an empty implementation for providerStateChanged, though in a real-world application you'd generally want to take some action:

```
        public void providerStateChanged(LocationProvider provider, int newState) {
                // Do nothing for our application
        }
```

The implementation of locationUpdated is taken directly from the run method of
LocationHandler. Add a timestamp to the message so you can see the location being
updated in the application. Also check to see if there were previous coordinates (if the
history isn't empty) and display the distance between the current set and the last set of
coordinates. First, add the following imports to LocationHandler.java to bring in the
date/time and coordinate-handling classes:

```
import net.rim.device.api.i18n.SimpleDateFormat;
import java.util.Date;
import javax.microedition.location.Coordinates;
```

The locationUpdatedMethod follows:

```
        public void locationUpdated(LocationProvider provider, Location location) {
                QualifiedCoordinates qualifiedCoordinates =
location.getQualifiedCoordinates();

                screen.setLocation(qualifiedCoordinates.getLongitude(),
qualifiedCoordinates.getLatitude());

                String message = "Successfully got location at ";
                SimpleDateFormat simpleDateFormat = new SimpleDateFormat("HH:mm:ss");
                message += simpleDateFormat.format(new Date(location.getTimestamp()));

                if (coordinateHistory.size() > 0) {
                        Coordinates lastCoordinates =
(Coordinates)coordinateHistory.lastElement();
                        message += "\nDistance from last update:" +
lastCoordinates.distance(qualifiedCoordinates);
                }

                coordinateHistory.addElement(qualifiedCoordinates);

                message += "\nMethod:";
                int method = location.getLocationMethod();
                if ((method & Location.MTA_ASSISTED) == Location.MTA_ASSISTED) {
                        message += " Assisted GPS";
                }
                if ((method & Location.MTA_UNASSISTED) == Location.MTA_UNASSISTED) {
                        message += " Unassisted GPS";
                }
                if ((method & Location.MTE_CELLID) == Location.MTE_CELLID) {
                        message += " Cell Site";
                }

                message += "\nHorizontal (Longitude) Accuracy: ";

                message += qualifiedCoordinates.getHorizontalAccuracy();

                message += "\nVertical (Latitude) Accuracy: ";

                message += qualifiedCoordinates.getVerticalAccuracy();

                screen.setMessage(message);

        }
```

Coordinates have a handy built-in method that can calculate distance in mneters between two geographical locations. You use that here. The interval is ten seconds. Usually, the first acquisition of GPS satellites takes longer than that, but after that's done, subsequent updates can happen quickly.

> **NOTE:** `net.rim.device.api.i18n.SimpleDateFormat` is an easy way to format date/time values into strings. The output format is specified using a format string, where different letters specify different components of the date/time to display. For example, if you have a `Date` object representing August 12, 2007, 9:57 p.m, you can get the following representations:
>
> `EEEE, MMMM dd yyyy at HH:mm:ss` would give `Sunday, August 12, 2007 at 21:57`
>
> `hh:mm:ss a` would give `9:57 PM`
>
> `yyyy-MM-dd` would give `2007-08-12`
>
> A full explanation of all the format characters is available in the Javadocs for `SimpleDateFormat`.

The run method will change to optionally add the listener and to remove the code that updates the UI in favor of calling `locationUpdated`. Replace the current try/catch block in `LocationHandler.run()` with the following:

```
        try {
                screen.setMessage("Getting location...");
                LocationProvider provider =
LocationProvider.getInstance(criteria);
                Location location = provider.getLocation(-1);

                locationUpdated(provider, location);
                if (periodicUpdates) {
                        provider.setLocationListener(this, 30, -1, -1);
                }
        } catch (LocationException e) {
                screen.setMessage("LocationException occurred getting location:
" + e.getMessage());
        } catch (InterruptedException e) {
                screen.setMessage("InterruptedException occurred getting
location: " + e.getMessage());
        }
```

You have set the location provider for an update every 30 seconds.

Finally, change the update method in `LocationMainScreen` to call the new constructor:

```
        private void update() {
                LocationHandler handler = new LocationHandler(this, true);
                handler.start();
        }
```

Start the application, select Update, and leave the application running. You'll see the location updated every 30 seconds. If you're running on a real device, walk around a bit to see your location being tracked!

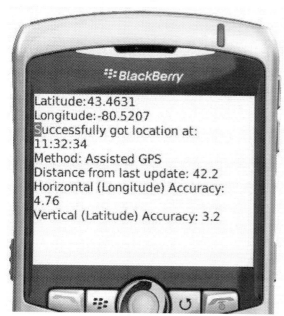

Figure 8-2. *Device location after a periodic update*

Using BlackBerry Maps

We've covered basic GPS location functionality. Now let's see how you can use BlackBerry Maps to display location in a more visual way.

BlackBerry Maps is included on devices running OS 4.2 and later, so it is available to most users. The API to interact with BlackBerry Maps is also available on any device that has BlackBerry Maps installed.

Prior to OS 4.5 an application could use BlackBerry Maps in a number of ways, including:

- Open BlackBerry Maps and display the default map view (the last map that the BlackBerry user viewed).

- Open BlackBerry Maps and display a custom map view (latitude, longitude, and zoom level).

- Open BlackBerry Maps and display a specific location (latitude, longitude, and zoom level) with a labeled marker.

- Open BlackBerry Maps and display multiple locations (multiple labeled markers on the same map).

- Open BlackBerry Maps to display a route between locations on a map.

With OS 4.5 and later, the API provides the capability to embed a map control into the UI of a BlackBerry application.

The Invoke API

The net.rim.blackberry.api.invoke package contains classes that let an application interact with some of the BlackBerry system applications, such as email, phone, and BlackBerry Maps.

Interaction is managed through the invokeApplication method of the Invoke class. This method takes two arguments: a flag indicating which application is to be invoked and an instance of an ApplicationArguments subclass specific to that application.

To launch Maps, you use something like the following:

```
MapsArguments args = new MapsArguments();
Invoke.invokeApplication(Invoke.APP_TYPE_MAPS, args);
```

Launching the Default BlackBerry Maps View

The previous code will in fact launch the BlackBerry Maps application with the default (last used) view opened. Let's add a new menu item and method to LocationMainScreen to do just that. Add the following imports to the top of LocationMainScreen.java:

```
import net.rim.blackberry.api.invoke.Invoke;
import net.rim.blackberry.api.invoke.MapsArguments;
```

Then, make the following changes to LocationMainScreen to add a menu item and a map method containing the previous code:

```
private void map() {
        MapsArguments args = new MapsArguments();
        Invoke.invokeApplication(Invoke.APP_TYPE_MAPS, args);
}

protected void makeMenu(Menu menu, int instance) {
        super.makeMenu(menu, instance);
        menu.add(new MenuItem("Update", 10, 10) {
                public void run() {
                        update();
                }
        });
        menu.add(new MenuItem("Map", 10, 10) {
                public void run() {
                        map();
                }
        });
}
```

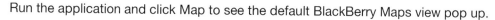

Run the application and click Map to see the default BlackBerry Maps view pop up.

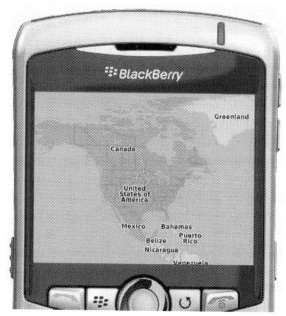

Figure 8-3. *Invoking the default BlackBerry Maps view*

This actually runs the Maps application and pushes the screen on top of y application. When you close Maps, you are back at the Location application's main screen.

Location Documents

BlackBerry Maps defines an XML document format that you can use to specify view information, location markers, and route information while invoking BlackBerry maps.

The basic format of a document showing one or more locations is:

```
<lbs>
<location y='latitude' x='longitude' label='Location_Label' description='Description'/>
<location y='latitude' x='longitude' label='Location_Label' description='Description'/>
<location y='latitude' x='longitude' label='Location_Label' description='Description'/>
....</lbs>
```

Each of the latitude and longitude values is an integer; you can multiply the decimal latitude and longitude by 100,000 to get the integer value.

Modify the Location application to take the list of coordinates in LocationHandler's history and map them when you select Map from the menu.

First, you need a way to get the list of coordinates. Add the following method to LocationHandler:

```
public Coordinates[] getCoordinateHistory() {
        Coordinates[] coordinates = new Coordinates[coordinateHistory.size()];
        coordinateHistory.copyInto(coordinates);
        return coordinates;
}
```

LocationMainScreen needs to have access to the location handler you invoke in the update method. You make it into a member variable by adding the following declaration to the top of the class:

```
private LocationHandler locationHandler = new LocationHandler(this, true);
```

Then, modify LocationHandler's update method to refer to this variable:

```
private void update() {
        locationHandler.start();
}
```

Next, you modify the map method to construct a map XML document using coordinates from LocationHandler. Remember that the x and y values for the locations are integers that you get by multiplying the decimal latitude and longitude by 100000:

```
private void map() {
        String document = "<lbs>";
        Coordinates[] coordinates = locationHandler.getCoordinateHistory();
        for (int i = 0; i < coordinates.length; i++) {
                document += "<location x='"
                        + (int) (coordinates[i].getLongitude() * 100000) + "'
y='"
                        + (int) (coordinates[i].getLatitude() * 100000)
                        + "' label='Location " + i
                        + "' description='Marker for history coordinate " + i
                        + "'/>";
        }
        document += "</lbs>";
        MapsArguments args = new
MapsArguments(MapsArguments.ARG_LOCATION_DOCUMENT, document);
        Invoke.invokeApplication(Invoke.APP_TYPE_MAPS, args);
}
```

One final thing before you try this; increase the time interval for location notifications to a couple of minutes or else you'll have a huge number of points located close together on the map. Change the appropriate line in LocationHandler.run to something like the following:

```
if (periodicUpdates) {
        // Update every 3 minutes
        provider.setLocationListener(this, 180, -1, 10);
}
```

Now, if you're up for it, load this on to your device, click Update, and then go outside and walk around for a bit. Then, click Map and you should see all your points displayed in BlackBerry Maps. The map view is automatically sized to display all of the points you give it.

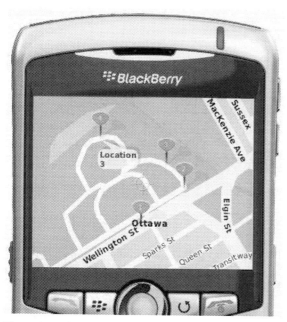

Figure 8-4. *Displaying a few locations in BlackBerry Maps*

Displaying a Custom Map View

In addition to letting BlackBerry Maps automatically position and zoom the view, you can specify a view in terms of a latitude, longitude, and zoom level.

To create a custom map view, you create an instance of `net.rim.blackberry.api.maps.MapView` with a latitude, longitude, and zoom. The zoom level ranges from 0 (zoomed all the way in) to `MapView.MAX_ZOOM` (zoomed all the way out). The view will be centered on the given latitude and longitude.

Let's add this functionality to our `Location` program. You'll first add a menu item to open a view zoomed in to 0 (all the way in) on the last updated coordinate.

Add the following import to the top of `LocationMainScreen`:

```
import net.rim.blackberry.api.maps.MapView;
```

Create a method called `customView` in `LocationMainScreen`; the code follows:

```
        private void customView() {
                Coordinates[] coordinates = locationHandler.getCoordinateHistory();
                if (coordinates.length > 0) {
                        MapView view = new MapView();
                        Coordinates lastCoordinates = coordinates[coordinates.length -
1];

                        view.sctLatitude((int)(lastCoordinates.getLatitude() * 100000));
                        view.setLongitude((int)(lastCoordinates.getLongitude() *
100000));

                        view.setZoom(0);
```

```
                          MapsArguments args = new MapsArguments(view);
                          Invoke.invokeApplication(Invoke.APP_TYPE_MAPS, args);
                 }
        }
```

MapView expects latitude and longitude in the same format as the location XML documents—an integer that is the latitude or longitude from the GPS location multiplied by 100000. We use another constructor for MapsArguments, which takes an instance of MapView and invokes the BlackBerry Maps application the same way. Finally, modify makeMenu to add a new menu item to invoke the customView method:

```
menu.add(new MenuItem("Custom View", 10, 10) {
        public void run() {
                customView();
        }
});
```

Now try it out and you should see a zoomed-in view of your last location.

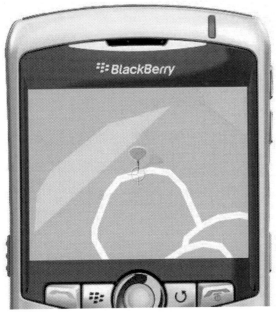

Figure 8-5. *BlackBerry Maps zoomed all the way in to our last location*

MapField: Embedding BlackBerry Maps in Your UI

From OS 4.5 and above, the BlackBerry platform provides the capability to embed a BlackBerry Maps view into your application's user interface.

You will add a map field to the user interface and have it update whenever a new location update happens. Because this works only with JDE v4.5 and higher, be sure that you're running an appropriate version of the JDE or that you've set your Eclipse workspace to use JDE v4.5 or higher.

The MapField lets you set a map position, but it doesn't support adding location markers to a map. So, you need to center the map on the new longitude and latitude and zoom in to maximum (level 0).

Add the following import to the top of LocationMainScreen.java:

```
import net.rim.device.api.lbs.MapField;
```

Add a new member variable for the MapField at the top of LocationMainScreen:

```
private MapField mapField;
```

In the constructor, initialize MapField. MapField enables you to set a preferred width and height using the setPreferredSize method. If you don't use this, the MapField's preferred size will be the size of the display, so just choose 200 x 100 and center it horizontally. Make the following modifications to the bottom of LocationMainField's constructor to place the MapField just above the RichTextField:

```
mapField = new MapField(MapField.FIELD_HCENTER);
mapField.setPreferredSize(200, 150);
add(mapField);

messageField = new RichTextField();
add(messageField);
```

Finally, modify LocationMainScreen.setLocation to set the mapField's location and zoom level whenever you get a location update. Remember, you have to multiply latitude and longitude by 100000:

```
public void setLocation(double longitude, double latitude) {
    synchronized(UiApplication.getEventLock()) {
        longitudeLabel.setText(Double.toString(longitude));
        latitudeLabel.setText(Double.toString(latitude));
        mapField.moveTo((int)(latitude * 100000), (int)(longitude * 100000));
        mapField.setZoom(0);
    }
}
```

Now run the application. Before the first location update, you'll see a map field with diagonal lines, indicating that it's set to an invalid location. Click the Update menu item, and when the location comes through, the map field should be centered on that location.

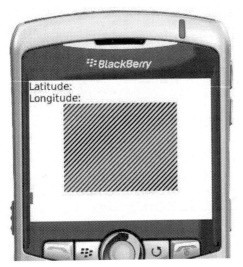

Figure 8-6. *Embedded map field before setting a location*

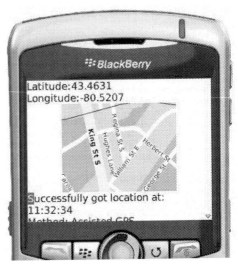

Figure 8-7. *The embedded map field after getting a location update*

Unlike BlackBerry Maps, the MapField doesn't support location makers. You can replicate this functionality (and do a lot more) by subclassing MapField and overriding the paint method. The convertWorldToField and convertFieldToWorld methods let you convert between latitude/longitude and pixels onscreen.

Summary

In this chapter, we covered the basics of location-based services on the BlackBerry. You built an application that retrieved the current location from the device's GPS receiver, and then extended the application to receive automatic periodic location updates. Then, you explored the BlackBerry Maps API, enabling you to plot the location updates on a map. Finally, you looked at the MapField, which enabled you to embed a map control into the applicaton's user interface.

There's more functionality available from location-based services on the BlackBerry, such as BlackBerry Maps, which can map locations based on street address and determine routes between two locations. We encourage you to take a look at the Javadocs and developer guides and explore more.

You now have the basic knowledge to make your application location-aware, opening up all kinds of new possibilities. At this point, we've explored as much of the BlackBerry API as we're going to in this book. In the next and final chapter, we talk about how to package and distribute your application to users.

Chapter 9

Getting Your App Out There: Packaging and Publishing

Now you know the basics of using the BlackBerry API to develop applications. This chapter is going to be a bit different. The best application is only successful if people actually use it, and to do that, they have to be able to find it and install it onto their BlackBerry devices. Of course, I've talked about signing your application and loading it onto a device using the command-line `javaloader` utility, but that was only to allow you to continue to explore BlackBerry development.

Until recently there have been a few main ways of installing an application onto the BlackBerry:

- *Over the air*: The app is downloaded using the BlackBerry browser from a web site on the Internet or your intranet.

- *Desktop*: The app is downloaded to the user's computer and, using the BlackBerry Desktop Manager, is loaded via a USB cable onto their device.

- *BES push*: In corporate environments, the BES administrator remotely installs an application onto the devices of some users.

Recently, a new way of installing apps debuted and is fast becoming the preferred method for distributing BlackBerry applications: BlackBerry App World.

In this chapter, we'll talk about both over-the-air and desktop installation, what you need to do to enable your app to be distributed in those ways, and what to look out for. Installation via BES push requires configuration by the BES administrator and a lot of knowledge about BES administration and so is outside the scope of this book.

We'll also talk about BlackBerry App World—how to set up an account, how to submit and manage an application, and what licensing options are available and how they affect your application's design. In addition, we'll explore some of the App World API that's available to allow your application to interact with App World in very useful ways.

We'll also briefly explore a couple of other leading third-party sites for selling and distributing your application.

Setting Application Properties

We touched on this in Chapter 2 by setting the title of the project, but when you're deploying an application to end users, you generally want to at least have a title and version (and probably vendor and description). Using the Eclipse plug-in, you can access properties by right-clicking the project name, selecting Properties, and then clicking BlackBerry Project Properties (Figure 9-1).

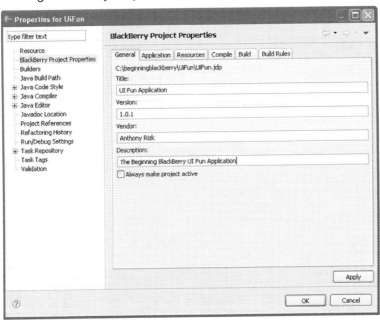

Figure 9-1. *Setting application properties in Eclipse*

Using the JDE, you can access application properties by right-clicking the project name, selecting Properties, and clicking the General tab (Figure 9-2).

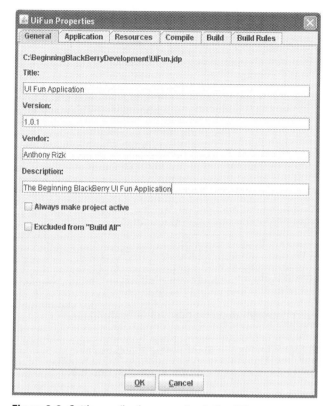

Figure 9-2. *Setting application properties in the JDE*

These properties will be visible to users installing your application over the air or via Desktop Manager, so it is important to fill them in with something that makes sense.

Over-the-Air Installation

The BlackBerry browser can be used to install a BlackBerry application from any web site that's accessible from the BlackBerry. For the most part, this means anywhere on the Internet or the corporate intranet if the device is activated on a BES. This is called *over-the-air* (OTA) installation.

Sibling COD Files

BlackBerry applications are compiled into COD files (with the extension `.cod`). When a compiled application contains more than 64KB of code or static data (including, among other things, resource files and static string data), the BlackBerry compiler breaks the COD file up into two or more COD files, naming them in increasing numerical order. For example, if we add bunch of images to our UiFun application, the COD files would be named as follows:

```
UiFun.cod
UiFun-1.cod
UiFun-2.cod
UiFun-3.cod
...
```

The compiler then takes these COD files, which are known as *sibling COD files*, and adds them all to a zip archive, which is then named the same thing as the first COD file: UiFun.cod.

The point of all this is that if a user is trying to download a COD file OTA containing sibling COD files and isn't connecting through the BES/MDS, the application will fail to install.

So, what we have to do in this case is unzip the main COD file and deploy all the sibling COD files to the web server instead. The steps for our example would be as follows:

1. Rename UiFun.cod to UiFun.zip.

2. Using a zip file program or the built-in Windows support for zip files, unzip the COD files.

3. Deploy the unzipped COD files to the web server—not the original zip file.

Note that if step 2 fails with a message that the zip archive is invalid, then you don't have sibling COD files and can safely deploy the single COD file to the web server.

The JAD File

Over-the-air installation requires a descriptor file called a *Java application descriptor* (JAD) file, which is a structured text file with the extension .jad.

Both the JDE and the JDE Plug-in for Eclipse generate JAD files automatically with your build. The JAD file will be named the same thing as your base COD file name, but with a .jad extension.

Since a JAD file is just a text file, you can use any text editor to change the contents.

Here's an example UiFun.jad file:

```
Manifest-Version: 1.0
MIDlet-Version: 1.0.1
MIDlet-Jar-Size: 395389
RIM-COD-URL-3: UiFun-3.cod
RIM-COD-SHA1-3: ff fb 53 97 7d 45 55 46 4b 0b 62 b5 8c 64 22 72 89 12 0f 4f
RIM-COD-URL-2: UiFun-2.cod
MicroEdition-Configuration: CLDC-1.1
MIDlet-Jar-URL: UiFun.jar
RIM-COD-Module-Dependencies: net_rim_cldc
RIM-COD-SHA1-2: a3 43 1d c9 fa b3 dc 74 af 9c 96 ea 8a 30 55 84 dd 0d 39 8e
RIM-COD-URL-1: UiFun-1.cod
RIM-COD-SHA1-1: 04 02 d3 d0 ef a3 1a 88 b5 bd a5 c1 9d b6 23 d6 9d 52 00 37
RIM-COD-Size-3: 29240
```

```
RIM-COD-Size-2: 56696
RIM-MIDlet-Flags-1: 0
RIM-COD-Size-1: 54096
RIM-COD-Module-Name: UiFun
MIDlet-Name: UiFun
RIM-COD-Size: 60208
RIM-COD-Creation-Time: 1250882363
MIDlet-1: UI Fun Application,,
RIM-COD-URL: UiFun.cod
MIDlet-Description: The Beginning BlackBerry UI Fun Application
RIM-COD-SHA1: b4 6b f1 d5 91 88 4a 8e e5 6a 40 8a 7b 12 5d 93 d1 20 bb 44
MicroEdition-Profile: MIDP-2.0
MIDlet-Vendor: Anthony Rizk
```

You can safely change a few of these values in the file—including `MIDlet-Vendor` and `MIDlet-Description`—but generally it's better to let the development tools take care of it. Later we'll see another way of generating JAD files using Apache Ant.

Content Types (MIME Types)

Before being able to download an application OTA from a web server, the web server needs to send the correct content types, or MIME types, along with the JAD and COD files. Table 9-1 describes these types.

Table 9-1. *MIME Types*

File Type	MIME Type
JAD	`text/vnd.sun.j2me.app-descriptor`
COD	`application/vnd.rim.cod`

How you set these types varies depending on your web server—consult your server administrator or hosting provider for more information.

Uploading Your Application

The last step to complete the setup of your OTA download is to upload your JAD file and your COD files to your web server. Make sure that your JAD file and COD files are all accessible at the same level of the web server. For example, if your JAD file is available at `http://www.mycompany.com/UiFun.jad`, the COD files should be available at `http://www.mycompany.com/UiFun.cod`, and so on. Users will only have to worry about the location of the JAD file, but the BlackBerry will need to access all the COD files as well.

Downloading the Application

Once all of these things are taken care of, you just have to open your BlackBerry browser and enter the URL to the `.jad` file into the web address field, and you will be shown a page that lets you download the application to your device (Figure 9-3).

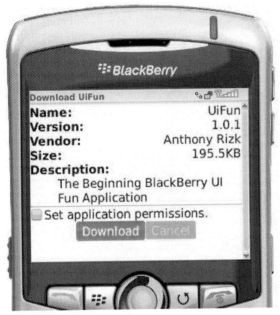

Figure 9-3. *Over-the-air download—notice the application properties we set earlier.*

Desktop Installation

BlackBerry applications can be installed from a computer to a device using a USB cable and the BlackBerry Desktop Manager. For large applications, desktop installation may save wireless data costs, and downloading an application is a lot faster over a broadband Internet connection than a 2.5G network connection. There may also be cases where wireless data access is not available on a BlackBerry device—if a user hasn't subscribed to a data plan or an IT policy forbids certain types of network access from the BlackBerry device. Generally, though, desktop installation is more complex and involves more steps than OTA installation, making it more difficult for users.

Unlike OTA installation, you don't have to worry about sibling CODs with desktop installation.

The ALX File

Desktop installation requires a different type of descriptor file than OTA installation. For desktop installation, the file is XML based and has the extension .alx.

Here's an example ALX file for UiFun:

```
<loader version="1.0">
    <application id="UiFun">
        <name >
            UI Fun Application
        </name>
        <description >
            The Beginning BlackBerry UI Fun Application
        </description>
        <version >
            1.0.1
        </version>
        <vendor >
            Anthony Rizk
        </vendor>
        <copyright >
            Copyright (c) 2009 Anthony Rizk
        </copyright>
        <fileset Java="1.39">
            <directory >

            </directory>
            <files >
                UiFun.cod
            </files>
        </fileset>
    </application>
</loader>
```

The ALX file format allows you to support more complex installation scenarios, such as different COD files for different devices. This is outside the scope of this book, but documentation is available on the BlackBerry Developer Zone.

To generate an ALX file using Eclipse or the JDE, right-click the BlackBerry project and select Generate ALX file (Figure 9-4 and Figure 9-5). The file will have the same base name as your project.

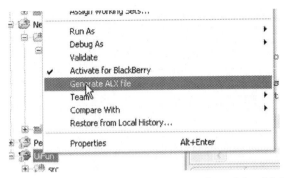

Figure 9-4. *To generate an ALX file from Eclipse, right-click the project and select Generate ALX file.*

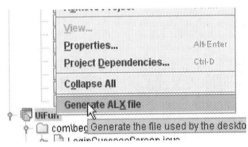

Figure 9-5. *To generate an ALX file from the JDE, right-click the project and select Generate ALX file.*

Distributing an application for desktop installation is easy—just give the ALX and COD files to the user.

The process of installing is a bit more complex:

1. Connect the device to the computer using a USB cable.

2. If it's not already running, start the BlackBerry Desktop Manager.

3. Select the Application Loader.

4. Click Add/Remove Applications.

5. Click Browse, and find the ALX file for your application.

6. Make sure the check box next to your application is checked (Figure 9-6), and click Next and complete the wizard.

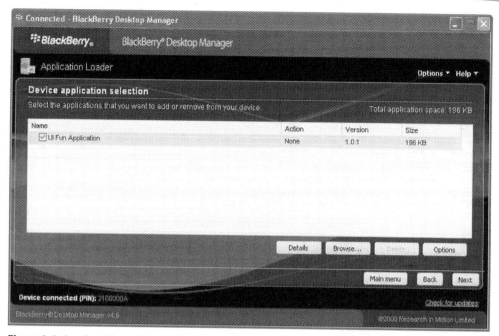

Figure 9-6. *Loading UiFun onto a device using the Application Loader from the Desktop Manager*

BlackBerry App World

In April 2009, BlackBerry launched BlackBerry App World—an on-device and web-based BlackBerry application store (Figure 9-6). App World is already the best way to distribute almost all BlackBerry applications. It offers a way for users to find applications, install them, and purchase them. Fortunately for developers, App World also takes away a lot of the headaches of deploying applications, making it easy to manage updates, deploy multiple versions for different devices and OS versions, and accept payment.

Figure 9-7. *BlackBerry App World*

Getting an App World Account

The first step in deploying your application on App World is signing up for an account.

Prerequisites

Whether you intend to sell applications or just deploy them for free, you'll need a PayPal account—a Personal, Premier, or Business account will work fine. App World processes payments in USD. To sign up for PayPal, go to http://www.paypal.com.

You will also require some documentation to validate the company information you provide (address and company name), or if you're applying as an individual, you will be e-mailed a statement of identification that must be filled out and signed by a certified notary.

The sign-up fee for App World is $200 USD. This allows you to submit up to ten applications.

Signing Up

If you're ready with the prerequisites, sign up for App World, and go to the App World Vendor Portal at https://appworld.blackberry.com/isvportal/ (Figure 9-8).

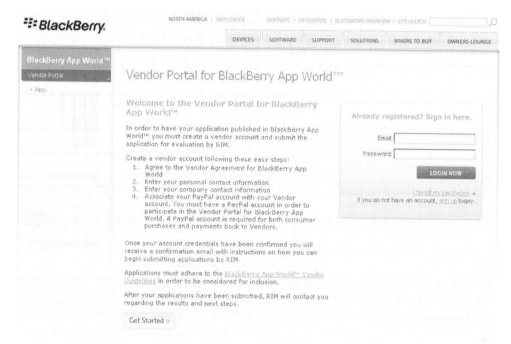

Figure 9-8. The BlackBerry App World Vendor Portal

Click the Get Started button, and follow the steps. You'll be asked to create one account when you sign up but can create more (if you want to let more than one person manage your applications) once your account has been activated.

If all goes well, you'll receive an e-mail shortly after either asking you for more information or informing you that you're now able to submit applications to App World.

Distributing Your Application on App World

App World applications are all managed through the Vendor Portal. Before we walk through an application submission, let's talk a bit about pricing and licensing.

Licensing Options

Applications on App World can be one of the following three types:

- Free
- Paid
- Try & Buy

Free applications are just that—free. The user pays nothing to download and use the application.

Paid applications require the user to pay a price that you set before downloading the application to their device.

Try & Buy applications allow the user to download the application free, but the user can pay to get a license key that either unlocks additional functionality or prevents the application from expiring (the actual functionality is up to you—App World just manages selling and distributing the license keys).

Paid and Try & Buy applications can be set up to use four different types of license models:

- Static
- Single Key
- Key Pool
- Dynamic Key

With the Static model, a license key is not required—when the user purchases the app, they download the unlocked version. For Try & Buy, this means you'll upload both a trial version and a full version of your application. This means you don't have to worry about a license key algorithm, but users must download another copy of your application when they buy.

With the Single Key model, there is one license key for all copies of the application. When the user pays, they receive this license key that they can use to unlock the application. It's simple but with one license key—anyone who gets the key can unlock your application.

With the Key Pool model, you provide a list of up to 2,000 license keys to App World, and these are handed out one at a time to each user who purchases the application. The advantage of this over the Single Key model is that you can track users by license keys, so if a key is being passed around, you may be able to deactivate or otherwise deal with it. To use the Key Pool model, you need to produce a text file, with one license key per line, to upload to App World along with your application.

With the Dynamic Key model, the App World server contacts your web server when a user has purchased the application and a new key is needed. Your server can then generate the key based on information about the application and the user's PIN or e-mail address. This lets you produce a key for each user, so there's much less danger of anyone else being able to unlock the application, but it requires more work on your part—hosting a server capable of responding to license key requests.

Implementing License Keys

What should a license key actually do? The simple answer is "It's up to the applicaton." That is, your license key just makes a trial application into a full application. What "trial" means is up to you.

For example, you may develop an application that

- Stops working after 30 days unless a license key is purchased

- Enables only certain functionality until a license key is purchased

- Disables some functionality after two weeks unless a license key is purchased

- Works only for a certain time period (for example, five minutes) or for a certain amount of data

License Keys for Try & Buy Apps

When a user purchases a Try & Buy application, they'll be shown a dialog box with their license key in the App World client. They'll be able to copy this key to the device clipboard, and you should provide a way for them to enter the key into your application to unlock it. Something as simple as an EditField will work. App World also automatically injects the license key into your application after it has been installed. See the "App World API" section later in this chapter for more information about how to retrieve this key from your application.

License Keys for Paid Apps

If you have to pay for a Paid application before downloading it, why would you want to provide a license key? Well, it's still useful for tracking purposes, and as we'll see later, App World will inject the downloaded application with the license key in a way that lets your application retrieve it later. If you choose a nonstatic license model for your application, the user will see a dialog box with your license key after they've purchased and downloaded your application.

Pricing

Applications for sale on App World—both Paid and Try & Buy—can priced in the following pricing tiers (all amounts are in USD but will be converted to the appropriate currency for the App World user):

- From $2.99 to $19.99 in $1 increments (i.e., $2.99, $3.99, etc.)
- From $19.99 to $99.99 in $10 increments ($19.99, $29.99, etc.)
- From $99.99 to $599.99 in $50 increments ($99.99, $149.99, etc.)
- From $599.99 to $999.99 in $100 increments ($599.99, $699.99, etc.)

App World takes 20 percent of the purchase price, giving 80 percent to the developer—not a bad deal for not having to deal with payment headaches, distribution, and so on.

The Submission Process

This section is a bit different from the other walk-throughs earlier in the book. Because we're dealing with a real, online submission process (with money involved), you shouldn't follow each step literally using the same app name. Rather, look at this as a step-by-step guide and insert your own application information where appropriate when you're ready to submit your BlackBerry application to App World.

The submission process will time out if you sit at any step without doing anything for ten minutes, so you may want to read through this section before submitting to make sure you have all the information prepared beforehand.

Starting the Process

Log into your App World account through the Vendor Portal, click Manage Applications, and then click the Add Application button. There are seven steps to the submission process

Step 1: Export Control

The questions here are to determine whether your application is bound by any export restrictions due to use of cryptography. Many applications do—all I can say is to answer truthfully here. If you think there may be problems with your application using certain types of encryption and being used in certain geographic areas, then you already know more information than I can give you.

Step 2: Main Application Data

You'll need to provide a few things:

- Your application's name (ideally you have that by now).

- A 480 × 480 pixel PNG image. This image should be the same as your application's icon; it will appear, scaled way down, next to the application names in the App World category lists (Figure 9-9). It will also be used as the archive icon if your users decide to archive your app to their SD card. This means that making this image different from your application icon will confuse your users. It also means you should avoid any very fine detail that might be lost when the image is scaled down.

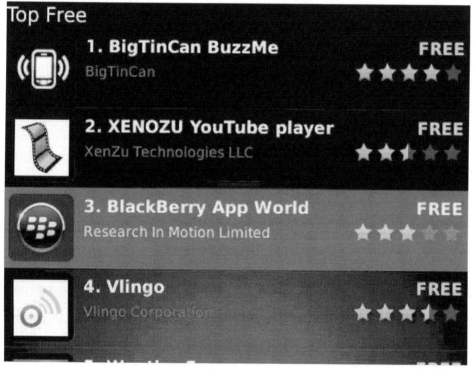

Figure 9-9. *Browsing the top free apps; the icons are scaled-down versions of the 480 × 480 pixel PNG.*

> **NOTE:** You probably have noticed the large images in the featured applications section of App World (see Figure 9-7)—those are submitted through a separate process, if you're lucky enough to get your application featured.

- The category and subcategory your application should belong to. These should reflect your application accurately, because a lot of users will discover your app by browsing through categories looking for an application for some specific purpose.

- The license type and license key information if required, as we discussed earlier, unless your application is free.

- The price for your application, again unless it's free.

Step 3: Description

The description can be a maximum of 2,000 words, and you must at least have an English-language description. You may provide descriptions for a number of other languages as well. If you do not submit a localized description, your application description will default to the English description.

Step 4: Distribution

You can choose to have your application available on some or all wireless carriers and in some or all countries. If you have exclusive agreements with some carriers or other reasons to restrict distribution of your application, this section makes that easy to manage.

Step 5: Screenshots

Screenshots can be up to 640 × 640 pixels, and you can provide up to 16 of them. The simulator is a great way to get screenshots of your application—from the Edit menu, choose Save LCD Snapshot.

Step 6: Releases

This is another area where App World saves you a lot of distribution headaches. The Releases section allows you to define each of the releases of your application that you want to make available on App World. When first submitting your application, you will probably have only a single release, for example 1.0, but later you can add more releases. App World will automatically distribute and notify the users of the latest release of your application.

With the bundles, you can provide different versions of your application for different device types, OS versions, or both, and App World will ensure that the correct version is installed on the correct device.

Don't worry about extracting sibling CODs—App World will take care of that for you. You don't need to provide a JAD file or anything other than the COD files for your application.

If you want to automate the release process more, App World lets you import all the information for a release from a zip file. This is handy if you want your build system to take care of updating the list of supported devices and OS versions for each build.

Different Versions for Different OS Versions and Device Models

There are cases where you may want to have several versions of your application available, such as if you want to leverage some OS 4.7–specific features to take full advantage of the Storm's touch screen but still want a version that supports all devices with OS 4.2.1 and later. This is easy to handle through App World using file bundles. We'll use a couple of examples to illustrate how this can work.

The first example is a version for OS 4.7 devices and a version for OS 4.2.1 devices:

1. Create a bundle called OS 4.2.1.

2. Check Supports All Devices.

3. Set the minimum OS to 4.2.1.

4. Upload your OS 4.2.1 COD file.

5. Create another bundle called OS 4.7.

6. Check Supports All Devices.

7. Set the minimum OS to 4.7.0.

8. Upload your OS 4.7 COD file.

App World will direct devices with OS 4.7 and later to the OS 4.7 version and will direct other devices to the OS 4.2.1 version.

The second example is a specific version for only the Pearl models, such as if your application needed a custom build for a small screen device and another version for all other devices. Follow steps 1–4 from example 1 to create an OS 4.2 version, then perform the following steps:

1. Create a bundle called Pearl.

2. Set the minimum OS to 4.2.0.

3. Uncheck Supports All Devices, and move all the 81xx and 82xx devices to the Supported box.

4. Upload the Pearl COD file.

This is how you can use the bundle distribution system in App World to provide specific builds of your applications for specific device models or OS versions.

Step 7: Summary

This summarizes the main data from your application submission. You can go back to any step by clicking the appropriate step in the header.

Done

And that's it! Your app will generally be approved in 8–10 business days and ready to distribute or sell to every BlackBerry device with App World installed.

App World API

App World also supports some API calls that let you integrate your application with App World in some useful ways. To help you get the most out of publishing on App World, we'll explore a couple of these features now.

Getting App World Properties for Your Application

App World embeds a number of properties in applications that are downloaded and purchased
through App World; these properties include the license key (if a license model other than static was used), the App World application name as specified in the Vendor Portal, the e-mail of the application purchaser, and others. Through the BlackBerry API, your application has access to these properties, so, for example, you can easily display license information to the user or pass license key information to your server as a way of tracking unique users.

The following code snippet will read a property set by App World from an application on the BlackBerry device:

```
    private String loadProperty(String appName, String propertyName) {

CodeModuleGroup group =
CodeModuleGroupManager.load(appName);
if (group!=null) {
return group.getProperty(propertyName);
        }
        return null;
    }
```

The appName parameter should be the same as the name you specified for your application in the App World Vendor Portal. The propertyName parameter can be one of the following string values:

- RIM_APP_WORLD_ID: The numeric ID of the App World application. This is useful if you want to launch the App World client to your specific application details screen, such as when an update is available or a trial has expired and you want to make it easy for your user to purchase your application.

- RIM_APP_WORLD_UPDATE_AVAIL: "True" if an updated version is available on App World, "false" otherwise. You may want to check this property periodically and have your application display a message to the user when an update is available.

- RIM_APP_WORLD_LICENSE_KEY: The license key (if any) associated with a Paid application or a Try & Buy application after the user has purchased the application and received a license key.

- RIM_APP_WORLD_NAME: The name of the application as specified in the App World Vendor Portal.

- RIM_APP_WORLD_EMAIL: A hash of the e-mail address of the purchaser.

- RIM_APP_WORLD_PIN: The hexadecimal value of the device PIN this application was downloaded onto.

- RIM_APP_WORLD_VERSON: The application version as specified in the App World Vendor Portal.

So, for example, to load the license key for an application named My Application that was purchased through App World, you would call the loadProperty method as follows:

```
        String myAppLicenseKey = loadProperty("My Application",
"RIM_APP_WORLD_LICENSE_KEY");
```

Launching App World from Your Application

With OS 4.3 and later, you can use the javax.microedition.content package to launch App World from your BlackBerry application and display a specific application when it launches. This is useful if you want to provide links to other applications you have developed or provide a way from your app to
easily open App World for a user to purchase your application after a trial has expired or download an updated version.

The following code will launch App World and open the application whose ID is provided:

```
import java.io.IOException;
import javax.microedition.content.ContentHandler;
import javax.microedition.content.ContentHandlerException;
```

```
import javax.microedition.content.Invocation;
import javax.microedition.content.Registry;
import net.rim.device.api.ui.component.Dialog;

public class AppWorldLauncher {
    public void launchAppWorld(String appId) throws IllegalArgumentException,
            ContentHandlerException, SecurityException, IOException {

        Registry registry = Registry.getRegistry(
SampleApplication.class.getName());

        Invocation invocation = new Invocation(null, null,
                "net.rim.bb.appworld.Content", true,
                ContentHandler.ACTION_OPEN);
        invocation.setArgs(new String[] { appId });

        registry.invoke(invocation);

        Invocation response = registry.getResponse(true);
        if (response.getStatus() != Invocation.OK) {
            Dialog.alert("Unable to launch App World");
        }
    }

}
```

appId is the numeric application ID given when your application is submitted to the App World Vendor Portal. You can find this ID when you click Edit on your application details in the App World Vendor Portal.

Other Application Stores

App World is certainly getting most of the press these days, but one of the great things about BlackBerry is that it's an open platform—as we've seen, you can post your app on your own web site, and there are several other application resellers that you can use besides BlackBerry App World. We'll mention a couple of the leading ones briefly, what they offer, and how you can publish your application through them.

MobiHand

MobiHand sells applications for most mobile devices, including BlackBerry. It also operates branded application stores for many other leading BlackBerry-related sites such as BlackBerryCool (http://www.blackberrycool.com), BerryReview (http://www.berryreview.com), BBGeeks (http://www.bbgeeks.com), CrackBerry (http://www.crackberry.com), and others. All of this means that MobiHand has a large audience and can help get your application noticed by more users.

MobiHand also produces an on-device app store client, called App Store for BlackBerry, which operates in a similar way to BlackBerry App World—though it's not quite as elegant. It allows users to search and browse applications, descriptions, and reviews and ratings, and it opens the mobile version of the MobiHand (or affiliate) web site for download and purchase of the application through the BlackBerry browser.

Signing Up for a MobiHand Account

You can sign up for a MobiHand account at http://corporate.mobihand.com/sda_dev.asp.

You'll need much the same information as for an App World account, including your company's name, address, and other relevant information. A MobiHand developer account is free, and you should be approved within about 24 hours.

MobiHand sells applications for devices other than BlackBerry, so if you plan to sell for other platforms, indicate that in your submission. Obviously that is outside the scope of this book!

Submitting and Managing Applications

The developer portal for MobiHand and all its associated stores is located at http://www.mobireach.com. When your account is activated, log into the portal, and select Products ➤ BlackBerry from the navigation bar to go to a list of your BlackBerry products (Figure 9-10).

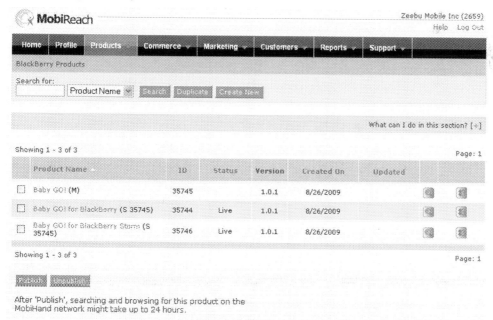

Figure 9-10. *The MobiHand developer portal showing BlackBerry applications*

Rather than walk through a whole application submission, we'll just discuss the options you have.

Product Types

There are three general types of product listings:

- *Standard*: Just a normal application listing.

- *Master*: A listing containing only pricing and application description information but no application—this is the method to handle applications with different builds for different device and OS versions. Master products are never directly listed on MobiHand.

- *Slave*: A listing containing information specific to a build of an application. The application must be associated with a master, so you need to create the master beforehand. These are listed on MobiHand with a name that's a combination of the master name and the slave differentiator. If your master is named My Applicaton, specify your slave differentiator as something like "for Storm" to have the product listing "My Application for Storm" listed on MobiHand.

Pricing

You can set any price you want for your application. Leave the price field blank for free applications. Prices are specified in USD and automatically converted to the other supported currencies, but you can override these conversion amounts.

You can also set a promotional price, with an expiry date, to enable you to have limited time sales on your applications.

Product Features

MobiHand will automatically determine which devices your application supports based on what you choose (you can manually change supported devices later). Even if you plan to manually change things later, it's a good idea to be as accurate as possible here so that when new devices are added they'll be handled correctly with minimal intervention on your part.

Activation

MobiHand supports several registration models, including free, paid, and a number of licensing models.

Additional Selling and Pricing Features

MobiHand provides some powerful tools to help support different sales strategies, including bundling applications together for one price, cross-selling (discounting later application purchases if a customer has purchased one application), and coupons.

Other Sites

Two other sites that you may want to look at as additional places to distribute and sell your applications are Handango (http://www.handango.com) and Handmark (http://www.handmark.com). Both—like MobiHand—sell software for a range of mobile devices, not just BlackBerry, and both may help you get your application into the hands of more users.

Summary

In this chapter, we've finished our introduction to the world of BlackBerry development by learning how to get an application distributed and loaded onto users' BlackBerry devices.

We looked at the basics of distributing an application on your own—including OTA downloading and loading via the BlackBerry Desktop Manager. Then we looked at BlackBerry App World, which lets you easily distribute your application and provides a way for users to pay for it. We explored the App World APIs that let you integrate your BlackBerry application with App World's functionality in a number of useful ways. Finally, we discussed third-party application stores, including MobiHand and others.

We're now very nearly done. You now know enough to get started building the next world-beating BlackBerry application. The next and final chapter will point you to a few additional resources that you may find useful as you continue to explore and build your knowledge of BlackBerry application development.

Chapter 10

Next Steps

We've come quite a way since starting out on our journey. You may have started with little or no knowledge of how to develop BlackBerry applications, but by this point you should be familiar with the basics of developing user interfaces and creating applications that use—among other things—persistent storage, wireless networking, and location-based services.

At this point, you're more than ready to start building the application of your dreams, but of course there's always more to know. The BlackBerry platform has been around for a while and has changed quite a bit in that time. It continues to evolve today—like the rest of the mobile world—at a faster pace than ever. BlackBerry App World is the first of many great additions to the platform that will come to the platform in the next while.

Mobile application development is still in its infancy, and BlackBerry is going to be around and growing with the mobile industry for a long time. So, part of your job as a BlackBerry developer will be staying on top of everything that happens, learning and evaluating new platform capabilities, and seeing if the new features would make your applications even better.

Keeping Up-to-Date

The main source for up-to-date information about BlackBerry is the first one I mentioned in this book, the BlackBerry Developer Zone:

`http://www.blackberry.com/developers`

Along with being the source for all your BlackBerry application development tools, the Resources section contains a lot of useful information and should be among the first places you turn to get a question answered:

`http://www.blackberry.com/developers/resources`

Among other things, the knowledge base, developer documentation (including development guidelines, white papers, and online versions of the Javadocs), tutorials, and videos are all very useful.

Forums

Several useful developer forums exist. The first one to check is the official BlackBerry Support Community Forms—specifically the Developer Forum:

```
http://www.blackberry.com/developers/forum
```

This forum is very active, and if you can't find an answer there, posting a question will usually at least let you find someone else who's had the same problem.

In addition to the official forums, a couple of third parties host fairly active developer forums, including BlackBerryForums:

```
http://www.blackberryforums.com/developer-forum/
```

Newsletters, Blogs, and Other Resources

All developers should subscribe to the BlackBerry Developer newsletter. It's free and delivers a new issue monthly:

```
https://www.blackberry.com/DeveloperUpdates/
```

A couple of useful blogs are also available. RIM in the last couple of months has launched its own BlackBerry Developer's Blog:

```
http://www.blackberry.com/developers/blog
```

This gives you the inside scoop from developers at RIM about a variety of development topics.

The Inside BlackBerry blog can also be useful for general happenings with BlackBerry:

```
http://blogs.blackberry.com
```

Finally, I maintain a blog called Thinking BlackBerry:

```
http://www.thinkingblackberry.com/
```

The official web site for this book is also a good source for source code for all the examples, errata, and other recent information:

```
http://www.beginningblackberry.com
```

If you can't find an answer to your question, contact me through either of those last two sites, and I'll do my best to help solve your problem!

Farewell

That's all! Thanks for reading all this way, and best of luck with all your BlackBerry development in the future!

Index

M